LANGUAGE AND LITERACY SERIES
Dorothy S. Strickland and Celia Genishi
SERIES EDITORS

The Complete Theory-to-Practice Handbook of Adult Literacy:
Curriculum Design and Teaching Approaches
Rena Soifer, Martha E. Irwin, Barbara M. Crumrine,
Emo Honzaki, Blair K. Simmons, and Deborah L. Young

Literacy for a Diverse Society:
Perspectives, Practices, and Policies
Elfrieda H. Hiebert, Editor

The Child's Developing Sense of Theme:
Responses to Literature
Susan S. Lehr

The Triumph of Literature / The Fate of Literacy
English in the Secondary School Curriculum
John Willinsky

The Child as Critic: Teaching Literature in
Elementary and Middle Schools, THIRD EDITION
Glenna Davis Sloan

Process Reading and Writing:
A Literature-Based Approach
Joan T. Feeley, Dorothy S. Strickland,
and Shelley B. Wepner, Editors

Inside/Outside: Teacher Research and Knowledge
Marilyn Cochran-Smith and Susan L. Lytle

Literacy Events in a Community of Young Writers
Yetta M. Goodman and Sandra Wilde, Editors

The Politics of Workplace Literacy: A Case Study
Sheryl Greenwood Gowen

Whole Language Plus: Essays on Literacy
in the United States and New Zealand
Courtney B. Cazden

The Social Worlds of Children Learning
to Write in an Urban Primary School
Anne Haas Dyson

Partners in Learning:
Teachers and Children in Reading Recovery
Carol A. Lyons, Gay Su Pinnell, and Diane E. DeFord

The Languages of Learning:
How Children Talk, Write, Dance, Draw,
and Sing Their Understanding of the World
Karen Gallas

THE LANGUAGES of LEARNING

How Children Talk • Write • Dance •
• Draw and • Sing
Their Understanding of the World

Karen Gallas

Teachers College, Columbia University
New York and London

Published by Teachers College Press, 1234 Amsterdam Avenue
New York, NY 10027

Library of Congress Cataloging-in-Publication Data
Gallas, Karen
    The languages of learning : how children talk, write, dance, draw, and
sing their understanding of the world / Karen Gallas.
        p.   cm. — (Language and literacy series)
    Includes bibliographical references and index.
    ISBN 0-8077-3306-7. — ISBN 0-8077-3305-9 (pbk.)
    1. Children — United States — Language.   2. Verbal behavior.
3. Communication in education — United States.   4. Education,
Elementary — United States.   I. Title.   II. Series: Language and
literacy series (New York, N.Y.)
    LB1139.L3G34   1994
    372.6 — dc20   93-36505

ISBN 0-8077-3306-7
ISBN 0-8077-3305-9 (pbk.)

Printed on acid-free paper

Manufactured in the United States of America

03   02   01   00   99   8   7   6   5   4

Contents

for Kelsey, Liam, and Dave

Acknowledgments

In 1985, when I returned to Massachusetts and knew that I wanted to return to the classroom, I found that few, if any, school systems were interested in hiring me to be a classroom teacher. Because I had my doctorate in education, I was considered to be unsuitable for work with children. One administrator even wondered out loud whether, after taking so much trouble to study education at a higher level, I would be able to withstand the confines of the classroom. Finally, Ralph Toran, an assistant superintendent in Norwood, Massachusetts, hired me to start a program for the gifted and talented, and thus began my journey back into the life of the school. For two years, Dr. Toran supported all my efforts to work with children whom we broadly defined as "gifted and talented," and those children helped me to become clearer about how I wanted to teach all children.

In 1987, personal circumstances intervened to send me looking for a classroom position once again, and, as before, I was met with little interest from administrators in different towns, with one exception. Nathan Purpel, then the principal of the Lawrence School, believed me when I told him that I truly wanted to teach first grade, and he took what was, for him, a calculated risk. The work I describe in this book is the result of his trust in my ability to "withstand the confines of the classroom" and his consistent and positive support for my teaching and my research.

Teacher research, however, is not easily done in isolation. In 1989, I stumbled upon the recently established Brookline Teacher Researcher Seminar, and I joined immediately. The members of that group have provided collegiality, friendship, support, and encouragement. Their dedication to their profession as well as their keen intelligence and fierce love for children are integral to sustaining this kind of work. Special thanks go to all of them: Steve Griffin and Sarah Michaels, co-founders of the seminar, Ann Phillips, Cindy Ballenger, Catherine O'Connor, Cindy Morton, Emily Woodbury, Jim Swaim, Joan Rector, Susan Black, Betsy Kellogg, Kim Williams, Vicki Morse, Sara Buswell, and Eileen Landay.

The work that began with my entry into the Seminar focused primarily on science talks and was propelled forward to a great extent by the

interest and enthusiasm of Sarah Michaels. Sarah's questions and prod-
ding, the clarity with which she approached children's language, and her
openness to many meanings were contagious. Further, Sarah's work on
sharing time prompted me to take it seriously as a point of study, and as I
did so, Steve Griffin and Cindy Ballenger also initiated important work
on children's communal talk. The thinking presented in this book on that
topic certainly began to develop, and continued to gain clarity, through
discussions with Steve and Cindy. In the same way, it took more than a
year of teacher talk for me to begin to write about bad boys. In that year,
Emily Woodbury, Ann Phillips, and I groped around for ways to talk
about "bad boys." Those conversations, their questions, and their personal
observations amplified my ability to speak about this difficult subject.

As the conceptual framework for this book emerged, several individuals contributed to its development in ways they might not have imagined.
Two former student teachers, Karen Kleinkopf and Kelly Demers, both of
whom were graduate students in the Creative Arts in Learning program
at Lesley College, in Cambridge, Massachusetts, collaborated with me on
curricula and ideas that are presented in this book. Karen's enthusiastic
work on the Egyptian curriculum helped to propel the children's interests
forward. Kelly, a musician as well as a teacher, taught me a great deal
about ways to work with vocalizing as well as the deep personal origins of
song and performance.

There were other fortuitous interventions: Nancy Madden, a parent
at the Lawrence School, gave me the book *The Songlines* (Chatwin, 1987)
as a gift one day, saying that she knew I ought to read it. I had taught
two of her sons, and obviously she knew something I did not. That gift is
proof of Nancy's perceptive nature. My reading of *The Songlines* deepened
my thinking on the nature of evolutionary intelligence and enabled me to
begin speaking about it in this book.

Other individuals have extended my thinking in different ways. Bob
Callahan's analysis of the place of chaos and alchemy in education helped
me to clarify my thinking about confusion. A long association and friendship with Shaun McNiff has deepened my understanding of the art experience and introduced me to the field of archetypal psychology. Shaun's
close reading of the manuscript, and his support of its point of view, were
invaluable.

Other readers have offered important insights and suggestions, most
notably Ann Phillips, ethnographer of the Brookline Seminar, and one of
the founding members. Ann's deep understanding of teaching and children, her careful use of language, and her unwavering belief in the importance of teachers' work have forced me to become clear about my own
work in the classroom. Her broad and careful thinking about theory has

been provocative at every stage of my research, and it was she who first encouraged me to write about my work in the *Harvard Educational Review*, thus beginning the process of writing this book.

Finally, special thanks to Sarah Biondello of Teachers College Press for her support of this kind of work, to Carol Collins, also of Teachers College Press, for her intelligent reading of my manuscript, and to my sister, Stephanie Gallas, for her strong support of the imperative to speak in the teacher's voice. Thanks also to my colleagues at the Lawrence School for their interest in my research and writing and for the insights they continually offer about the art, and the labor, of teaching. Their constant search for professional growth and renewal along with their willingness to share their knowledge continue to stimulate and expand my understanding of teaching and classroom practice.

Of course, there would have been no book without the children. Beginning with my own children, Liam and Kelsey, and moving outward, hundreds of young children have alternately delighted and confounded me, but they have always provoked wonder, imagination, and awe. Thanks to all of them. And thanks to my husband, Dave Edwards, for supporting every aspect of my work and making it impossible *not* to write.

If the word "text" is understood in the broad sense—as any coherent complex of signs—then even the study of art . . . deals with texts. Thoughts about thoughts, experiences of experiences, words about words, texts about texts.

Mikhail Bakhtin (1986)

Introduction

My mother must not have gone to the same kind of school you went to. 'Cause she doesn't know how to speak any of those languages you speak.

Natalie, age 6

Thus Natalie stopped me in my tracks on her fifth day in my classroom, forcing me to sit down on my steps and wonder how a 6-year-old child, homeless and in her first week of school, could understand so much. Even after she was removed from our school a week later and sent to live in another town, her words followed me and forced me to think more clearly about the powerful role that language plays in constructing the history of so many children's lives, about how my access to many "languages" of learning had made my life more privileged than others, about how the classroom has the potential to help children, all children, "speak in tongues" — and in so doing move to broader and more powerful ways of presenting themselves to the world.

This book is about speaking in tongues, about how children can be urged to exercise their natural proclivity to interpret language freely and use that potential to expand and develop as learners. It labels this kind of expansive language as *narrative* and explores what an expanded definition of *narrative* might mean in the classroom.

This book is also about children's thinking. It builds on the work of Bruner (1986), Cazden (1988), Hymes and Cazden (1980), Michaels (1990), and Wells (1986), among others who have cited the importance of narrative as a source of knowledge for children, but pushes the definition of *narrative* further and considers it broadly — as a "complex of signs and texts" that make children's thinking visible. In doing this, I propose that important texts are obtained through the rich dialogues that children so eagerly engage in with one another, with me, and with the world at large. To a great extent, the notion of narrative presented here fits within the framework of "prosaics" as conceptualized in the work of Bakhtin (cited in Morson & Emerson, 1990). Within that context, "a model of language . . . is nothing unless it can help us to appreciate the overlooked richness, complexity and power of the most intimate and ordinary exchanges" (p. 34).

THE POWER OF STORIES

For children, meaning is built into stories; they use narrative to construct mental models of their experience, to make the world they inhabit sensible. Because narrative is sometimes narrowly viewed as having to do with stories or storytelling, and thus is confused with fiction, it is sometimes thought of as only an aesthetic or literary experience. Yet narratives can be true or false, or both, and in fact, as Bruner (1986) points out in his description of literary narratives, "stories of literary merit . . . are about events in a 'real' world, but they render that world newly strange" (p. 24). So, too, narratives about real life in many cases also serve to "render that world newly strange," to make it larger than life, to imbue it with a meaning that goes beyond the circumstances of the event itself.

We all tell stories about our lives to point out something that has consequence for us. The degree of consequence is greater in some cases than in others, but I believe that children are more acutely sensitive to the nuances of their lives. They take greater notice of unusual events, and they use impressions from all aspects of their experience to form personal narratives that attempt to explain and order their world. These personal narratives are often part of the silent language that embodies thinking. As Merleau-Ponty (1964) says, "all language is indirect or allusive — that is, if you wish, silence. . . . we must uncover the threads of silence that speech is mixed together with" (pp. 43–46).

It seems very important that children have a place where seminal experiences, which occur both in and out of school, move from silent expression into speech. I am reminded of my observations of my own young children as they encountered new experiences in the world: their isolated wanderings, for example, on a remote island off the coast of Maine. They would return home silent, but filled with deep thought. What might they have realized if their school had been one where they could have shared their observations and thinking with others, where their silent narratives would have been made manifest and weighted with recognition? Children's narratives, if uncovered and honored in the context of the classroom, can become powerful vehicles for thinking and learning.

EXPANDING THE DEFINITION OF NARRATIVE

In the process of recognizing the power and importance of narrative functions, we must also expand our definition of *narrative* to include much broader realms of communication and expression. In this book, I present a conceptual framework which suggests that for children in schools, deep, transformative learning takes place when *language* is defined expansively to include a complex of signs. Children's narratives are not naturally confined to the spoken or written word. From early childhood on they tell stories in dramatic play, in their drawings and paintings, in movement and spontaneous song. As they move further into the adult world of signifying, spoken language does begin to take precedence, but in essence children do not *naturally* limit the forms that their expressions take. Because adult communication relies so heavily on spoken and written language, however, schools necessarily reflect that orientation and channel children's narratives into a very narrow realm of expressions, in effect limiting rather than broadening the child's expressive capabilities.

What if we were to assume that children came to school more, rather than less, able to communicate their thinking about the world? Why not assume that when the child enters school, he or she presents us with an enormous number of innate tools for acquiring knowledge and, rather than considering them to be "constraints" as Gardner (1991) suggests, consider them to be assets? What effect might this assumption have on our approach to what the languages of learning are? If we liken children's flexibility of mind to the infants' flexibility of body, the analogy becomes clearer. Infants can put their toes in their mouths, and they show immense flexibility in their joints and spines when they roll over or lounge on their backs. It is logical to assume that the mind also has a similar flexibility, that initially it is capable of tapping into processes of thinking and communication that are far more varied and interchangeable than the spoken word, processes that we have at birth but gradually lose from lack of use.

The capacity to represent thoughts within melodic phrases, for example, is a form of symbolization most of us rarely employ. In the book *The Songlines* (1987), Chatwin describes the belief of aboriginal Australians that the world was sung into existence—a *poesis* that continues in the present as aboriginals sing their way across the land on their walkabouts. In this process, "each totemic ancestor, while traveling through the country, was thought to have scattered a trail of words and musical notes along the line of his footprints" (p. 13). As the tradition continues today, the ancestral songs re-create creation, allowing members of each aboriginal community to describe the ancient paths across the continent. In the songlines, the melodic lines represent the contours and paths of the journeys, and the lyrics tell the stories of creation. This ancient practice by a large population redefined for me the symbolic boundaries of song; it prompted me to go back and rethink my past observations and encounters with children, to remember my young children singing as they played, and to recall my son's question at 10 years of age—"Mummy, there are songs in my head; what should I do with them?"

At that time, I was barely able to help him with a question that was clearly an urgent one, as he recalled how the songs kept him awake at night and filtered through his thinking during the day. I remember thinking that he must be expressing some sort of special musical gift, and I urged him to play those songs out on our piano or sing them to me. Those suggestions fell far short of the question he was asking, a question I now define differently. Now, each night before I sleep, I listen to the melodies in my head. They are not always known tunes, and I cannot understand how to make them available to myself as information. As I make note of the songs on the edges of consciousness and in my dreams, I am able to reflect on what these "texts" might signify about my own knowledge of the world. More importantly, I wonder about their origin, and then suppression, over the course of my own life.

What then, is the natural predisposition of the human mind for symbolic representation of thinking? What kinds of powerful capacities for reflection and reorganization of our mental experience are we, as teachers, unable to tap into with children because we have irretrievably lost access to them, thus limiting their use as potential tools for intellectual and creative growth? Finally, what might the potential for thinking, learning, and being look like for our children if, over the years, their entire education provided opportunities for them to expand, rather than narrow, their range of expressive and narrative functions?

Over the years spent with adults who are less flexible in their thinking and communication, most children lose their natural gifts for narrative expression. However, these gifts remain active and productive in the lives of artists, who, through intent or for purposes of survival, manage to remain versed in a vast array of expressive strategies. That we relegate the adaptive use of song, movement, painting, sculpting, drama, and poetry to a small segment of our population does not confirm that those areas of expression are available only to a few—only that those few have made a conscious choice to live their lives immersed in other ways of being. When children are continuously offered opportunities to express their stories about the world through many avenues, they show that the power and range of their intellectual and creative pursuits are unbounded; they create new kinds of learning communities that offer membership to every child; they teach us that the process of education transcends methodology and curriculum and is situated in the realm of possibility. They change our conceptions of who teaches whom in the classroom. Once we begin to understand the many paths that narrative can take through the modalities of talk, song, art, and movement into the written word, the practice of teaching and the process of learning are mutually transformed.

The use of narrative, however, embodies a serious epistemological dilemma for teachers. Who is to determine what is true and what is not, what has been learned or taught and what has not, and who has learned or not learned it? Much of the work in the classroom is driven by these questions. When narrative is conceptualized as a window from which to consider such questions, the process of education becomes more complex. Recognition of narrative as a legitimate and powerful way to describe the world essentially admits that stories about the world are subjective and only represent the teller's perspective. As Bruner (1986) says, "Story must construct two landscapes simultaneously. One is the landscape of action . . . the other of consciousness: what those involved in the action know, think, or feel, or do not know, think or feel" (p. 14).

Narrative introduces the factor of human subjectivity into the process of describing what has or has not taken place in the classroom. In effect, its use forces the teacher and child to listen, watch, and speak in the first person. New elements enter into conversations about learning. There is the temporal interaction of the participants. There is the story, poem, picture, or performance that points to deeper metaphoric meanings, thus expanding the temporal relationships. There is the aesthetic or literary element that the story points to, and there is the deep cultural and ontological knowledge that the allusion represents for all members of the community. The possibility of certitude and accurate "measurement" of learning is overtaken by what Brueggemann (1991) calls "the embarrassing footnote . . . to the canon of certitude . . . odd experiences of human transformation that are always minority reports in our capacity to 'get it right'" (p. 28). When narrative is used as a way to reexperience a reality or to redescribe a learning event, the text, whether it be poem, story, picture, or song, is not the actual event but rather a story about that event. All stories allow us to cast a different light on the event itself; all allow child and teacher to reenvision the process of learning and teaching in a way that defies standardization and objective description of what has been learned.

THE SETTING

The texts that are cited in this book reflect teaching and research I have done in my classroom in a semiurban public school setting over the past five years. During this time I have been both a first-grade teacher and a teacher of a combined first and second grade. The population of children I teach is diverse, representing many races and ethnic groups and all levels of the socioeconomic spectrum. Many of them speak English as their first language, but often as many as a third do not. My classroom, although situated in a public school, is unusual in its spatial arrangement. It is a product of the open space building trend that swept this country in the late 1960s and the 1970s; there are no windows, walls, or doors, only a series of steps that lead to a long and winding classroom area. The children in my class have access to many different kinds of spaces within the classroom, some of which are located on large wide stairs and some of which are on different levels.

It should also be noted that the classroom includes several different work and study areas, including a large wet area that at different times houses art activities, water play, and planting experiments; a block corner; an area for large-group meetings; a science and social studies corner; and different spaces that are stocked with particular kinds of materials ranging from writing materials to art and science supplies, manipulatives for math and reading, and a listening center. In addition, we have many different kinds of animals that live with us all year, some of which have played a role in many of the stories included in this book. They include Violet, our angora bunny, mated cockatiels, newts, salamanders, frogs, snails, slugs, earthworms, fish, and a variety of insects.

Throughout this book, I explore the different kinds of stories I have seen and heard in my classroom, describing both the development of those stories and the ways in which they have illuminated, or changed, my interaction with the children I have taught. The book opens with a description of how my work as a teacher-researcher evolved in response to the larger question of teacher stories and where the authority to speak about teaching and learning resides. That discussion continues contrapuntally within each chapter, superimposing my conversations with myself about teaching over my conversations with children about their learning.

The stories I relate are divided into three parts. The first, "Epiphanies of the Ordinary," focuses on the mundane in the classroom: those narratives that have the potential to be the glue holding a classroom community tightly together. The second, "Stories about Science," describes children's forays into the world of science within the context of spoken and written language. The third, "Art as Story," widens the discussion of narrative and places the art experience at the center of classroom life.

All three parts assert the primacy of expression and creative thinking as goals that serve all children, that push their boundaries of thinking and communication, and jostle the teacher's boundaries in much the same way. Each section speaks through different kinds of stories, yet each acknowledges the necessity of speaking in tongues as the anchor of the learning process. It is no accident that the term *speaking in tongues* emerged for me as an important description of the goal we strive for in the classroom. It signals the transformation that occurs when a community of learners realize that language is transcendent; that what may at first be unintelligible can be known when a new system of meaning-making is constructed. Thus the imperative that has emerged for me at every point in my research and teaching is the urgency of exploring the untapped potential for expression and learning that all healthy children bring with them to school. Clearly our knowledge of children's capabilities is limited not by a lack of effort in studying them, but rather by a limited vision of what we study, how we go about it, and in what terms it is discussed.

1

On Being an Aboriginal

A Model for Teacher Research

I try to keep my eyes open all the time,
remember as much as I can,
and not judge more than I can help.
Johann Wolfgang von Goethe (1962)

In 1927, Werner Heisenberg pulled out the rug and our whole under-
standing of the universe toppled and collapsed. . . . The Principle of
Indeterminacy . . . says in effect that you cannot know both a parti-
cle's velocity and position. You can guess statistically what any batch
of electrons might do, but you cannot predict the career of any one
particle. They seem to be free as dragonflies. You can perfect your
instruments and your methods till the cows come home, and you will
never be able to measure this one basic thing. The electron is a musk-
rat, it cannot be perfectly stalked. And nature is a fan dancer, born
with a fan; you can wrestle her down, throw her on the stage and
grapple with her for the fan with all your might, but it will never quit her
grip. She comes that way; the fan is attached. . . . As a consequence,
physicists are saying that they cannot study nature per se, but only
their own investigation of nature.
Annie Dillard (1974)

I like to think of teachers and children as the particles that cannot be
tracked as they career through space and time, elusive like the muskrat
and living within the Principle of Indeterminacy. Seasons change, humid-
ity fluctuates, chicken pox arrive, children are hungry. The barometer
falls, wars begin, the heating malfunctions, people die. Pets are lost, a
building is vandalized, the roof leaks, the gerbil dies. The snail has babies,
a sister is born, parents divorce, the teacher is sick. How can we study
and track the life of the classroom when that life embodies the dynamic,

changeable patterns of nature? What is educational research, is it ever "scientific," who has the authority to speak about classrooms and children, and in what voice?

Because the work I describe in this book falls outside the mainstream of educational research and represents a distinctly ethnographic approach to describing my classroom and the children in it, it is important to be clear about the issues of research, writing, and authority that have shaped my presentation of the stories from my classroom and that may affect the reader's appropriation of these stories. Thus, in this chapter, I would like to identify those things that distinguish a teacher-researcher from other researchers in the field of education. I do this with the knowledge that there is a debate going on about what efficacious research on teaching and learning is. The differences of opinion and of practice originate, I believe, in point of view.

Teachers tell stories about their classrooms. At their brief lunch breaks, in after-school gatherings and meetings, when speaking with new acquaintances, they transmit information about what they do through the story, or the personal anecdote (Phillips, 1992). In the story, the content almost always ties meaning to an emotive value. Useful stories, for teachers, are those that ring true, stories that are evocative of their own lives in the classroom. Each story we hear forces us to situate ourselves in relation to the personal truths that the storyteller is relating; each story, although not a fiction, presents many perspectives and many meanings rather than one focused and conclusive meaning. Teacher stories, although not cloaked in an attitude of knowing, are about what teachers know about children, learning, and teaching. They are often characterized by elements of surprise, conflict, and mediation, as well as what Bruner (1986) calls the subjunctive mode: "To be in the subjunctive mode is . . . to be trafficking in human possibilities rather than in settled certainties" (p. 26).

The language of most educational researchers, however, uses the tone of the academy and the explicit intent of science. It is distanced, authoritative, oriented toward wider meanings and generalizations, and often implies that there are right or wrong ways of teaching. It does not speak in the voice of uncertainty, does not acknowledge the changeable, instinctive, and intuitive character of teaching. It speaks of measurable variables and outcomes, and it is not a voice that teachers naturally recognize as speaking to them. The discourses of teachers and researchers are separate and thus promote separation. As Gee (1990) says, knowing a discourse allows you to belong to the club, but mastering the Discourse, with a capital D, requires more than just learning to read the language or speak correctly. Entry into the club of teachers or the club of researchers requires initiation, entitlement, and approval by the members of the club. It involves learning to think, act, and communicate in certain ways, and those ways embody more than an agility with language or social imitation. Those ways are ways of being in the world.

More specifically, mastering a discourse often signals a movement up (or, conversely, down) in the social hierarchy. For teachers, acceptance into the halls of the research community is a process of upward mobility, and they generally leave teaching, leave the physical and communal structure of the school, to make that transition. For researchers, I would characterize acceptance into the teaching community as akin to "going native." Members of the academy who move back into the classroom to do research rarely stay. The labor of teaching is hard, physically and emotionally draining, allows little or no time for reflection and recharging, and certainly implies a lower social status. They move in for awhile, participating as outsiders who have inside knowledge that will help the community they study move forward, as it were, into the next century, or teaching temporarily as insiders in order to study a particular phenomenon. Then they move out again, publishing their findings within their own community, and the teachers and children they once worked with become subjects to be discussed and evaluated. Very few people live with feet planted firmly in both worlds.

As I write this, I am unable to shake the image of ethnographers in the early part of this century "assisting" the aboriginals they were studying in emerging from the Stone Age culture they lived in. Any teacher who has attended national research conferences on education cannot help but come away with the feeling that she or he *is* an aboriginal. Every aspect of life in the community of the classroom is highlighted for study and discussion; and in those discussions, the person of the teacher is truly disembodied as a research subject. Even the stories teachers tell are studied as a curious sort of folklore that somehow represents a mythology about teaching.

As a first-grade teacher, perhaps I do represent some of the traits of an aboriginal. I speak of a child learning to read in magical terms. My colleagues do the same. While our methods, structure, and intent as teachers of reading imply a systematic approach, we know in our hearts that the event of reading is magical. When a child learns to read, we are awestruck — not knowing absolutely that any one thing we did so systematically caused that outcome. We know that the measurement of variables, coefficients, and reliability will not help us as teachers of reading. We know that one cannot measure or generalize about in absolute terms how the epiphany of reading happens for each child. Yet we all have important things to say to one another in our stories about what we have learned from the children, and those things can improve our teaching of reading.

This tacit understanding that teacher knowledge offers important insights is not formally valued and honored by most teachers because it is usually exchanged informally and because it receives little recognition by the educational research community for the contributions it makes to the improvement of teaching. Most teachers and administrators tend to view outsider knowledge about teaching as "real" knowledge that embodies true expertise about instruction, evaluation, and learning, and insider knowledge as somehow less important, perhaps because it is so accessible.

The research of individuals who are not involved in the day-to-day operation of a classroom, however, is rarely presented in terms that relate to the life of the classroom or that recognize the fluid way teaching and learning are constructed. Teachers attend workshops and take short courses in different "canned" methodologies (what I like to call "evangelical courses"), and do return to the classroom energized by the new ideas. What often happens, however, is that those ideas also go native after awhile, much as Christianity is eventually absorbed and changed by the native religions it purports to replace.

Thus, if I want to speak to my colleagues in schools about life in the classroom from a researcher's point of view, I must begin that journey from a very different point of origin than my colleagues in the academy. I must begin with the story. In the interest of furthering a conversation that will draw teachers and educational researchers closer together, I must carefully describe the process of teacher research as it has developed for me in the context of my classroom and my membership in a small teacher-research community.

SHIFTING FROM TEACHER TO TEACHER-RESEARCHER

Early in my teaching career, I developed an interest in exploring the potential of the creative art experience for teaching and learning. Specialization in a style of teaching, or an area of the curriculum, is not uncommon for many veteran teachers. At that time I began to collect paintings and drawings, and I recorded how the art experience assisted either the children or myself in expanding our horizons. For many years, I collected only children's artwork, realizing as I did how clearly the paintings and drawings revealed the child's mind. That work eventually led to a doctoral dissertation and a temporary break from classroom teaching.

Like many educators who receive advanced degrees, I believed that I could better serve the profession if I moved into teacher education, and so I spent four years teaching at the university level, supervising student teachers and thinking about education. Yet every time I visited a student in a classroom, I grew nostalgic. Everything in the classroom fascinated me, from the papers on the walls, to the materials on the shelves, to the smell of the building as I entered. Somehow the university classroom, where I taught about the practice of education, was disembodied and remote, representing more "the naked corpse of the word" (Bakhtin, 1981, p. 292) than the life of the classroom as I remembered it.

When the circumstances of my life intervened to enable me to return to the classroom, I walked in with a different perception of what was precious in teaching. Although my interest in the role of the arts continued and expanded, I also took greater notice of every classroom event, and I began collecting more things. After joining the Brookline Teacher Research Seminar in 1989, my vocation as a collector quickly became full-blown. I moved from collecting art, to audiotaping and transcribing children's discussions and interviews, to collecting everything that caught my eye.

Now I pick children's notes out of the trash, record bits of conversations on the playground, save junk sculptures, copy children's math calculations off the board, hoard their doodles, and record my own astonishment at recess antics. It seems sometimes, as I sort through the artifacts and field notes, that I am simply a compulsive collector of children's memorabilia. Yet although the process of gathering data may appear to be somewhat unsystematic, or even random, it is comparable to my more intuitive acts as a teacher, when I change direction in a lesson based on a child's look or gesture. Somehow I know to follow my instincts as a collector. Those things that I deem precious will inform me later on.

THE CLASSROOM AS A RESEARCH COMMUNITY

From my vantage point, then, teacher-researchers working with ethnographic methods are distinguished from most other effective teachers in this one important area: We purposefully gather data with which to reflect upon our teaching, our questions, and our children's learning. In the process of data collection, we take advantage of some very basic ethnographic research techniques that are especially suited to the classroom. We keep field notes, collect artifacts (samples of children's work), and use audio- and videotaping technologies. This process of data collection is ongoing. It becomes part of the life of the classroom and is absorbed into the interactions between teacher and students. Thus, over the course of a school year, I compile an enormous amount of information that helps me to reflect on the classroom and to answer my more difficult questions about teaching, learning, and the process of education.

Further, when I collect data as a teacher-researcher, my process differs in its point of origin and its place in the life of the classroom from that used in alternative assessment methods that also employ more qualitative tools such as the use of field notes and portfolios. As a teacher-researcher, I do not determine beforehand the categories of information I am looking for, the nature of the data, or the questions to be asked. Data collection is not a process used only for assessing children's learning or evaluating curricula. The process of data collection, as it has evolved, has become a central part of my classroom practice.

As I have become more involved in classroom research, my work has become more visible to the children I teach. Throughout the process of doing research in my classroom, I make it clear to my students that I am documenting *our* work. They become familiar with the tools I use and often assist me in using them. They expect the tape recorder to be on when we have discussions, and they often listen to and comment on the tapes. They expect me to have my notebook out when we are working on projects or doing a movement experience. They are not surprised if I photograph them or their work. They understand that while I am a teacher, I also study what is happening in the classroom. This, in fact, is a source of pride for them. It makes their actions as learners more important and more powerful. It also enables me to see each child's progress throughout the year more clearly; and even if the data remain in rough form, they provide a record from which to consider many questions about process, outcomes, and effectiveness.

Further, the children know that my study of the classroom results in writing and talking to others about our work. They question me about my work. "Do you have to do this?" they ask. "Don't you remember what you were like when you were a child? Why do people want to know about what kids think?" Their questions enable me to be more explicit about the kinds of things I want to understand, and I share my questions with them. I ask them, for example, to talk to me about "songs," about what science is, about what makes the composition of a dance "hard." They take my questions seriously, and in the process of trying to answer those questions, they think more deeply about their own thinking, and I am able to examine mine. Usually their answers take the form of short stories or narratives about their lives. As a teacher who also uses stories to explain what I understand, I observe that these stories make the child's mind clearer both to me and to the child. In effect, we are speaking the same language to begin with, and thus the story naturally becomes part of the way that I must speak about my research.

DEVELOPING A NEW RESEARCH MODEL

The style of this book reflects my conviction that in discussions of teaching and learning, narrative accounts best represent the process of education. This orientation continues the tradition of Elwyn Richardson, Sylvia Ashton-Warner, George Dennison, John Holt, and Herbert Kohl, to name a few, individuals whose narratives I read and was deeply affected by as a student of education. I now recognize that these teacher-writers left a legacy of inquiry and reflection that I have adopted in my practice. In this tradition, "the teacher's theorizing is a joint project of knowledge and confusion; in this research tradition one never finally knows" (Ballenger, 1993, p. 12). The process of writing and thinking about the classroom, then discussing it with colleagues, is saturated with a strange admixture of theory, convictions based on past experience, deeply felt emotion, missionary fervor, intuition, and qualified conclusions. As Clifford (1986) writes, ethnography is

> a performance emplotted by powerful stories. Embodied in written reports, these stories simultaneously describe real cultural events and make additional moral, ideological, and even cosmological statements . . . these kinds of transcendent meanings are not abstractions or interpretations "added" to the original "simple" account. Rather, they are the conditions of its meaningfulness. (pp. 98–99)

I know that my stories represent *my* version of classroom events. Hence the tentative nature of my authority as a transmitter of knowledge about the classroom; hence the qualification, the hesitation, the amazement, the sense that many achievements are magical.

As a teacher-researcher using ethnographic techniques to study classroom life, I find myself in a peculiar position. By using an ethnographic approach, I combine both dynamic and synoptic perspectives on the children I study. As the teacher, I stand inside each classroom event, witnessing *and* participating as it unfolds. As the researcher, I collect and analyze data, some of which has been directly influenced by my participation in the classroom I am studying. This dichotomy represents a tension that necessarily determines how I "read" my data, and the ways I write about them. The primacy of the story as the form that presents my data and in many ways personalizes its interpretation frames the research in a more distinctly allegorical way than that of other educational researchers.

Allegory does not pretend to be presenting the world from an objective standpoint. Rather, it takes on a symbolic and metaphoric tone in which I acknowledge that my stories are only presenting my picture of what happens in my classroom. That does not negate the power and realism of the stories, or the insights about children and classrooms they might contain, but it does require that I make no claims of generalizability or reliability for my findings. Clifford (1986) points out that once ethnographic stories are recognized as allegorical, "what formerly seemed to be empirical/interpretive accounts of generalized cultural facts . . . now appear as just one level of allegory . . . no longer *the* story, but a story among other stories" (p. 109).

Seen from this point of view, the act of writing moves from a clean, distanced, objective account toward a personally involved, evocative act. And, although this style of writing clearly embodies the ways in which teachers speak about the classroom and provokes powerful responses from teachers, at the same time it represents a genre that many researchers regard as particular and problematic. This genre is problematic for them precisely because it is not immediately generalizable, because it qualifies the knowledge it is presenting. Yet it speaks powerfully to teachers, urging them to consider the important insights they put forth in their own stories about children. The voice of the teacher-researcher embodies the tension between the teaching and research communities. It is like the Roman god Janus, looking in two directions: claiming authority as the guardian of classroom stories and abdicating it in the next breath.

Where should teachers look for authority in reflecting on their work? Do we look only to ourselves and our past experience as reference points in understanding the teaching and learning process? Do we rely solely on the theoretical premises of scholars and the research paradigms of educational researchers, many of whom have never taught children, or taught little? Or do we look both in and out, relying on our own instincts and our intuitive understandings of children, as well as on the body of knowledge that has come before us? My orientation toward narrative differs somewhat from the earlier style of teacher narratives I have cited, in that the act of writing about my classroom will locate itself both in my stories about the children I teach and in the theoretical and literary traditions that have helped me to think about the children and the dynamics of the classroom.

Beginning with Confusion

Although it is somewhat heretical for a teacher, especially an experienced teacher, to acknowledge her perception of chaos and personal confusion, let alone to tolerate it in her classroom (Phillips, 1992) that is a beginning point for research that will run throughout this book. Classrooms are supposed to be orderly and structured, and teachers are expected to have control and to direct the process of learning. However, my stance as a teacher-researcher often begins by situating itself in an attitude of not knowing and loss of control, not in a physical sense, but in the existential sense of losing control of the meaning of habitual practices.

Sometimes that attitude presents itself in a difficult question. Other times, however, even the question is elusive, prompting me simply to begin to look into the chaos or confusion that surrounds me. By recognizing that I do not understand what is happening, I acknowledge that, most probably, the chaos I perceive reflects more my state of mind than the logic of events in the classroom. Classroom events, in and of themselves, are purposeful and have an innate order. What is lacking is my understanding of that order. Thus the act of looking might be compared to the process of "clear seeing" or "beginner's mind" in Buddhism, in which one enters into the flow of events with an attitude of disorganization and openness, rather than organization and structure. In other words, the teacher looks into the life of the classroom with imagination, and without preconceptions that limit, rather than expand, his or her ability to understand. In some cases, the teacher even allows an unsettling event to unfold based on a wholly intuitive feeling that by not intervening, by allowing children fully to uncover their own stories and meanings, by, in fact, abdicating control of a situation and looking at it without an internal censor, new understandings can be gained.

This "looking" becomes organized for me in the process of data collection. By focusing the teacher's lens, collecting data gives me a point around which the confusion reconfigures itself so that patterns can emerge. However, the collection of data in relation to a specific question or to the admission of confusion about a phenomenon does not guarantee that the answer can be found. Because my stance as a teacher-researcher begins with acknowledgment of chaos and confusion, the answers to the question (and even the questions themselves) often remain unknown throughout the process. What follows and intertwines with the process of data collection is a continuous cycle of reflection and of questioning those reflections [or, in the terms of archetypal psychology, "seeing imaginally" (Hillman, 1975)], of looking at the data without boundaries so that the children, the teacher, the data, the process, and even the question are all constantly changing and rearranging themselves in different relationships.

Perceiving New Patterns

As a teacher-researcher, when I adopt an attitude of not knowing, of looking into the void, two distinctive things happen. First, patterns do begin to emerge, patterns that were most probably always present in that particular classroom but were not visible because my eyes were not really open. Second, I can move to the next stage of action, in which I acknowledge my previous inability to see and begin subtly to change my practice based on newly perceived patterns and on my realization of those limitations or biases that had prevented me from seeing into the chaos and confusion. However, within this new stage of reflection and then reaction, there is also the recognition that the understandings that come from the research are completely situated in time and place. What the teacher has perceived in one instance with one particular child or group of children cannot necessarily be generalized to another child or group of children. What can be generalized, though, is the extreme value of an attitude of not knowing, of accepting the presence of confusion, of attempting to look into that confusion with some sort of structure and purpose, even if the purpose is only to look.

It is inevitable that in the act of looking imaginally, the observer's stance in relation to the phenomenon being observed must change. As a teacher of children, I move from being sure of what I am doing and therefore doing it unselfconsciously, to being unsure and self-conscious. I move from probability to possibility. For the purposes of seeing, hearing, and perceiving children's meanings, I seek to expose my limitations as an interpreter of the world, rather than conceal them. In this process of viewing children's texts, teacher and child are mutually engaged in looking imaginally at the world. As I am increasingly more able to make sense of the vast languages of learning that children can so ably employ, then with the children I can identify in an ever-broadening sense what is being understood or misunderstood, what is known and unknown, and those questions still to be explored.

In this context, the use of narrative in this book becomes more important. As I have stated, narrative seeks to point or show something that is weighted in the narrator's life. Thus my stories about the classroom present a personal account of the process of research and those events that propelled that process forward. In many cases, I record the texts and present them in their raw, unedited form, giving the appearance of separating data from interpretation. That semblance does represent my stance as a participant-observer. Later, I retell that particular event from my own point of view in an attempt to understand its dynamics and meaning. Immediately, in the retelling of the story I lose all claims to objectivity, but in the retelling comes the illumination for me, the discovery, as it were, of what was sitting in front of me but had remained elusive. And further, in the process of telling my own story, I subtly alter my relationship to the children, and thus the process of teaching and learning is changed. Therein, of course, lies the tremendous power of teacher research.

In some cases, the stories document my journeys into understanding my own history as a learner, and they underscore how the legacy of a teacher's schooling lives on in her practice. Other stories describe my attempts to make sense of what I was seeing in the classroom, in effect documenting my struggles with not knowing, and they point to those patterns that began to emerge for me. In those, I try to situate myself within the body of knowledge that I have gained from the children as well as those theoretical works that enabled me to make better sense of my data.

All the stories show how children have expanded their use of different narrative forms, making their thinking apparent to both themselves and to me. My text, however, makes no claims about universal methods, validity, or generalizability to other teachers in other settings. It places itself outside of the dominant quantitative tradition of educational research, eschewing objectivity and distance from research subjects. It represents the very subjective view of a classroom teacher, and it asserts that powerful and important understandings emanate from the intimate and changeable relationships of the classroom, providing as proof "embarrassing footnotes" and stories that are grounded in amazement, metaphor, ambiguity, imagination, and, sometimes, pain.

If, in the process, I learn things about children that are new, contrary to prior research, or revolutionary, those are outcomes I have not anticipated. As a teacher-researcher, ultimately the process of inquiry begins with a question or with confusion. The journey I take to answer that question or see into the confusion often leads to places I never intended to go.

PART I

Epiphanies of the Ordinary

> *Worldmaking is learning in the widest sense, but it is also an adaptation to environment as nature, a search for higher levels of syn-thesis of self and world drawn from the recognition that outer and inner worlds are interdependent aspects of reality, rather than independent states.*
>
> *Edith Cobb (1977)*

Sometimes, in examining the most mundane of classroom events, one gains the greatest insights. "Talk is cheap," as the saying goes. It is one of those classroom events that is not considered to be an event. Rather it goes on continuously with seemingly few variations; it per-meates the life of the classroom. Part I begins with a consideration of the most commonplace kind of classroom talk: sharing time. In pre-senting this form as an important speech event, I hope to initiate a dis-cussion of the ways in which close attention to events that are not part of the formal teaching day enable teachers and children to build the underpinnings of a strong classroom community, to go about the important business of "worldmaking." Although the discussion opens in Chapter 2 with sharing-time talk, it expands to include other kinds of "texts" available to teachers: pictures, notes, conversations, and ob-servations in and out of the classroom.

As I reflect on my own initial interest in talk, I recognize that often what I choose to think about and reflect on as a teacher-researcher are the ways of communicating that were missing parts of my own education. Sharing time was one of those missing links. There is no question that it is one of the most commonplace daily oc-currences in the primary classroom, a part of every teacher's day that is embedded in routine. Although I am sure that I participated in sharing time, or show-and-tell, as a child, I have no recollection of that event, and in fact I cannot recall ever talking about what was important in my life within the context of the classroom.

I know now, after looking carefully at sharing time and trying to understand my own fascination with it, that what I needed as a child in school was a teacher who wanted to hear my voice, my ideas, the words that were always present but never spoken; a teacher who would have given me support and safety and a space in which to project that voice; a teacher who might have asked to hear my thoughts spoken out loud, who by asking me to talk without fear of judgment would have valued my voice just because it was mine, not because it provided the right answer.

As a child, I had no sense of what it meant to think out loud, therefore thinking for me was a solitary activity that could not be made better in collaboration with others and that certainly never took form in a speech event, an artwork, a dance, or a song. Those forms only became available to me when I started to teach, and they produced a miraculous transformation in me as an individual. I found that with children I could actually think out loud and they would respond, and I liked it. I liked being in that teacher's chair surrounded by children, controlling thinking with words, gesture, and theater. It was very powerful. Eventually I also found that the children's support gave me courage. I could even think out loud with adults, and it was no longer a terrifying experience.

It is also important to note that from the earliest point of my teaching career, I could only function in a classroom where children could talk their way through the day. The classrooms of my childhood had been silent. Friendships were formed outside of class and had nothing to do with the business of learning. Signs of intimacy, of close contact with other children, things such as note passing or a serious discussion with a friend, were forbidden. Thus in the 1970s, when I was a new teacher, allowing children to talk in the classroom was, in my opinion, my first rebellious act, directed at the goal of making classrooms more humane. As I thought more about the kind of classroom I wanted to have, however, the symbols of children's links to one another, rather than to me as their teacher, also became important. I wanted to hear them talking and laughing, settling small disputes, making art together, playing games, building things. In short, I believed that the classroom should reflect children's connections rather than their separation. It seemed only logical that that kind of environment would further their ability to embrace learning completely.

It is evident to me now that while informal exchanges among

children and teachers are a natural part of the life of the classroom, the existence of that kind of relaxed atmosphere alone is not enough. By paying explicit attention with the children to the many different ways we are using language, and to the many kinds of texts we are sharing, we all become more self-conscious and more capable as communicators. We acknowledge the many distinct discourses that the children must acquire to be successful in school: the discourses of science, math, literature, social studies, and the arts, of sports and the playground. Further, each year there is a slowly evolving discourse of each class of children, containing in it special words, themes, and references that reflect the interests, ethics, and common experiences of that class. It is to this discourse that children quite naturally pay attention; and I must be aware of it if I want to be an influential part of the classroom community, in effect acknowledging that the social, creative, and intellectual concerns of the children form a corpus that I must know and study in order to be an effective teacher.

This first section of the book presents ways of looking at children that focus on various aspects of the mundane in the classroom: talk, playground behavior, drawings in daily art journals, notes to friends, casual remarks made by children, simple observations of children as they go about the routine business of school, personal accounts of my interactions with a child. As a teacher-researcher, I view all of these events as data which can help me describe the children I teach; and all, when used to construct a picture of a particular child, become texts to consider. In the process of building a classroom community in which every child is valued as an important member, the data inform me. They tell me about the children, about how they are constructing their school personas, about their intellectual and personal concerns, about their strengths as learners, about those things that they find difficult, about their basic understanding of what schooling is, about worldmaking. It also tells me about myself, and enables me to verify or disprove my own gut reactions to classroom situations and particular children.

In writing about the process of defining a learning community, I present children and classroom phenomena that particularly interest me as a teacher-researcher. As I mentioned, Chapter 2 explores sharing time as a form of classroom discourse. Chapter 3 describes the journey of an immigrant child as she worked to become a part of our classroom culture, as well as my search for ways to teach her. Chapter 4 explores the world of "bad" boys, and their role within the classroom community. I believe that these descriptions illustrate the complex process that teachers go through to build a powerful, inclusive classroom community. Successful teachers develop curricula and structure classrooms by gleaning important information from many subtle and nebulous sources such as those I describe. Often they describe that process as one that uses intuition, as well as past experience, to make judgments and form strategies.

Intuition cannot be taught, it cannot be measured, it is hard to describe systematically and therefore hard to document. However, it is the foundation on which artful teaching is built. I use the term *artful* with the assumption that the artistic process is a complex system in which both critical and creative thinking are involved and in which intuition plays a major role. I hope in this section to reveal some of the sources on which the intuition in artful teaching is based and to show how teachers can begin to document those sources and collect more tangible and permanent evidence of the complex stories that children bring to school. Often, in the process of hearing and paying attention to those stories, teachers begin to see themselves more clearly as lifelong students of children's understandings.

2

Sharing Time
When Children Take the Chair

What is the value of sharing time in the primary grades? In the late fall of 1989, as I began to reflect carefully on the different kinds of talk in my first-grade classroom, and more particularly on my influence on classroom discourse, I had become uncomfortable with my role as the central figure in classroom talk. I decided, after three months of school, to implement a noninterventionist style with my sharing-time groups. I guess I was not really sure why at the time, but it seemed as if my presence in the center of sharing time was inhibiting the children's expressive potential. So I started to turn the sharing over to the kids. They sat in my chair, and I sat in the back of the audience and listened. It was fascinating from the start. The children simply adapted as if I had never been in the sharing dyad, and I observed, but did not document, the evolution of a completely new sharing format.

Early in the fall of 1990 I asked myself the question once again, but this time with more seriousness: What is the value of sharing time in the primary grades? Like most teachers, I had been taught to think that show-and-tell, or sharing, was an important time in the day when children could take center stage and bring something of their home life into school, a time when they were encouraged to speak publicly on topics of their own choosing. Truthfully, though, I had had little understanding of sharing time as a speech event, and I had also been a victim of the anomie that afflicts most primary teachers when faced with sharing time. Inside my head, it sounded something like this: "I know I'm supposed to do it, but it truly is so deadly boring and repetitive, and the children don't really say anything, but heck, I'm conscientious, so I'll grit my teeth and tolerate it." I had certainly thought this, and had had many teachers say the same thing to me, so I decided as part of my classroom research on language that I would try to clarify the "why" of sharing time.

I was curious about what would happen if I began the school year by turning sharing directly over to the children. How would the talk develop

17

once the model of a teacher-run, teacher-focused sharing time wore off? What would happen to a group of children when they spent time each day talking together about their lives, and what would I, in the process of documenting this event, learn about language and the children I taught? This class was composed of 22 children representing four different language groups and a range of socioeconomic backgrounds. As much as one-third of the class were not native English speakers, and the class was racially mixed, including 3 African-American children, 11 Caucasians, 6 Japanese, a South African black, and an Ethiopian.

Bernstein (1972), in discussing the idea of compensatory education, calls for the teacher to acknowledge each child's culture: "If the culture of the teacher is to become part of the consciousness of the child, then the culture of the child must first be in the consciousness of the teacher" (p. 149). Certainly sharing time is one of the few classroom events in which the child directly presents his or her culture. I understood that by examining sharing time, I would be responding on one level to Bernstein's challenge, but I also wished to expand the idea to include the notion of building a culture and community of the classroom. If the child is to participate fully in the community of the classroom, with its diversity of language and culture, then all members of the community, children and teachers alike, must participate and join in the community of each child.

Michaels (1990) talks about the ways in which "certain forms of discourse, certain ways of making and displaying meaning, often nonnarrative in nature, come to be privileged, promoted and 'taken' into children's talk and writing" (p. 306). She posits that the teacher's role in this is one of "ratification" of the texts, both spoken and written. In other words, the teacher, by virtue of both verbal and nonverbal support or denial of a discourse, transmits a very clear message about the types of communication that are appropriate for school.

By removing myself from the teacher's traditional role in sharing time, I could explore what happened when the children became the primary audience, or the "ratifiers" of the discourse. The notion of ratification, then, would be extended to include all members of our community, and in that process the children could expand everyone's conception of what effective narrative could be. As Michaels points out, in sharing time teachers promote literate characteristics that fit mainstream conceptions of what literacy and talk should be. However, this direction is not successful with all children. It follows, then, that a sharing community that privileges all kinds of talk, and in which every child's cultural membership is valued, should influence change in every child: African-American children will attempt to master mainstream talk, new immigrants will find acceptance for their efforts to communicate, and, conversely, as nonmainstream narratives are included, white children will attempt to master those genres.

A NEW SHARING STRUCTURE

Early in the year I introduced a structure in which I sat in the back of the audience and the sharing child sat in my chair. For the most part, every child chose to share on a regular basis. Each child had a designated day of the week when he or she could share. Generally, anywhere from two to five children would volunteer to share on a given day. The format was that when the child was through with the narrative, he or she would ask for questions or comments. I only participated in the question/comment portion of the sharing episode if no child had anything to say or ask. As the year progressed, the children learned that one had only to wait patiently and questions or comments would arise.

What happened over the course of the year was a remarkable series of transformations in the way that the children talked and listened to one another. In looking over my field notes and the taping of sharing sessions, which began in early October and continued through May, I was astonished at the complexity of the sharing process. My field notes contain observations on how this experience enabled bilingual children to be included in our community, how children came to understand the orchestration of group talk, how children found ways to listen and develop one another's narratives, how issues of entitlement and power were played out. They include observations about the role of the audience in the experience—that is, what it requires to be a good listener—and the role of the sharer; what the behaviors are that make one child more able than another, able in the sense of maintaining a sharing episode, or, as one of my 6-year-olds said, "keeping the chair as long as possible."

I recorded how the exploration of different kinds of narrative liberated some children and helped them finally to join into our community fully, and how it stretched the expressive capabilities of other very competent children. I could develop case studies of several children whose narrative skills were significantly expanded from September to June: children from other cultures, children who had difficulty expressing simple ideas because of early physical and emotional trauma, and very shy children who would never speak above a whisper. Finally, I could describe how the process of acting as a teacher-researcher has forever changed my own conceptualization of what sharing time can be. However, all of these themes and their ramifications for classroom practice are most clearly realized in the story of Jiana, who, in the enormous weight of her past and present and future, taught us all many things about language, teaching, and community.

JIANA

Jiana was 6 when she entered first grade in 1990. She was a tall, skinny African-American child who came to our class because she had moved into the shelter across the park from our school. Her mother had just returned to the family after six months of separation, and her father was in jail because of drug-related incidents. Jiana had been living with her grandmother in the spring and summer of 1990 and had apparently attended only a few months of kindergarten. When she came to us, her family had just begun the process of trying to reconstruct itself, but she was still in shock from the trauma that had occurred in her life. Although she entered school with great bravado, it soon became clear that academically she was functioning on a prekindergarten level. And because Jiana was physically very tall for her age, there was no way to avoid the issue of catching up. She had to catch up, but she was already so far behind the race that I knew it could not conceivably happen. She recognized only a few letters and numbers, could barely write her name, and had extreme trouble naming common objects, animals, and pictures. She appeared to have little, if any, experience with books. When she was in the classroom, she had one goal: to make friends, to just "be" in school. However, the act of "being schooled" was not part of her repertoire.

I soon found out, as we all began to talk to one another in group, that Jiana could hardly talk. She could not collect her thoughts clearly enough to get them out in a coherent way. Her speech was filled with stops and starts, long hesitations, and incredible difficulty in finding the words for simple objects and ideas. Often, when trying to make herself understood, she would have to stop and ask me, for example, "What's that thing? You know — the thing that you use to cut with?" And I would have to query her further to understand whether she meant a knife, scissors, a saw, or some other cutting instrument.

Two years earlier, before I had begun to think more carefully about how to make room in my classroom for many different language styles, I would have referred her for a speech and language evaluation as fast as possible. Her inability to express her ideas in the most simple of contexts would have frightened me into believing that she had problems that could never be dealt with properly in the classroom, with 22 other children needing my attention. However, because I now was able to recognize that

I had no grasp on the reality she brought with her to school — on her story, as it were — I felt compelled to listen and watch, to make the classroom a place that welcomed her and did not send her away. I decided to wait and see.

JIANA AND SHARING TIME

Jiana wanted to share from day one, and she always tried to participate in other children's sharing by asking questions and offering comments. When she got into the chair, it was as if she were sitting in a forbidden place. She would perch on the edge of the chair, with her long legs tucked neatly together. She would slouch her body to one side, put her finger to her cheek, and cock her head to think. Inevitably, she would look out at me, as if asking for permission, and I'd say, "Go ahead, Jiana." And then she would try to start. Her narratives were usually unintelligible, but she persevered. Here is an example of her talk in early October, when she was sharing a half-finished bookmark. (Each dot indicates a pause of one second in Jiana's talk. "Karen" refers to me.)

JIANA: I made this at LEDP [after-school program].
TEACHER: I don't think they can hear you, honey.
JIANA: I got this in LEDP, and . . . . . and I made it . . . . and I didn't want it so . . . . I'm going to give it to Karen.
TEACHER: Do you want to tell more before you take questions?
JIANA: Questions or comments? . . . . Fanny.
FANNY: What are you going to make it out of? What are you going to make it out of?
JIANA: I'm not gonna make it.
FANNY: But it's not finished . . . Well, you're going to have to show Karen how to do it because she doesn't know how to do it. And also, I think you need a needle for that.
JIANA: I know.
FANNY: Oh, do you have a needle?
JIANA: No.
FANNY: A fat one.

Jiana's language was very basic; the children drew her out. This was a trend that began early. As I sat in the back of the crowd and watched, other children, like Fanny, began to teach Jiana how to fill in her narratives.

And this sort of tutoring continued. Jiana would generally have very few material objects to share. She would bring in small coins, rocks from the playground, asphalt shingles that she had pulled off the side of the shelter. She would share her sight-word cards, reading them incorrectly to the class, but the children persisted in waiting through her long pauses and asking her questions about even the smallest issue, so that she could stay in the chair. I found this process terribly painful to witness. Often, as she struggled, I wanted to look away and preoccupy myself elsewhere, much as one might avoid looking at a handicapped person laboring to perform a simple function. However, although I secretly despaired that Jiana would never gain fluency, I was taping and listening carefully. Apparently my attention and silence in the midst of Jiana's long pauses led the children to believe that they should take care to try to follow Jiana, and they did.

After three interminable months, something happened. Jiana got into the chair and stated that she did not have anything to show, just something to tell. She described a trip to the aquarium that she had taken with the after-school program. I sat up. Something in her demeanor was different. She was talking loudly, sitting up straight in the chair, and actually listening to the questions and making follow-up comments that propelled the sharing forward. As the following excerpt shows, her narrative, although still filled with hesitancies and word-finding problems, was detailed and spirited. I was convinced that a change was taking place and that she had rehearsed this sequence.

JIANA: Oh. Um, and we saw the rainforest, we saw um, um, there was a um, thing on a, ... like a say, tree, and there was a . . . . . a fake snake, and everybody, and, and some it was a fake snake but it was long and somebody was moving it in back of the thing, and and everybody thought it was a snake and everybody screamed.

DONALD: Did you scream?

JIANA: No! Because . . . . . . 'cause, a a snake couldn't be . . . . yellow.

SEVERAL: Sure it could. It can.

JIANA: . . . And we saw, . . . and we saw um, ... little kinds of shells and we went to the pickup thing, where we pick up um, um, um, this big crab . . . . . . We get to pit it, pit it, we get to pit it up, and we pitted, picked it up, with some little things and they have a lot of legs.

SEVERAL: Starfish! Starfish!

JIANA: Yeah. Starfish.

In the weeks that followed, Jiana switched back to sharing objects and was again unable to form a narrative around them. Yet she had begun to expand her comments about other children's sharing into narratives about how her life was like theirs. For example, she told how she had cats, too, and she would give details of their antics (even though I did not believe many of her stories, and my attitude, my slight annoyance that she was fabricating stories would play itself out later). In making these comments, however, her inflection, intonation, and personal force would change; and the narratives often became a series of linked stories, which we would sometimes have to stop because they gradually increased in length.

One day shortly after the Christmas break, Jiana brought in a Christmas ornament to share. She sat in the chair and described it, explained that she had gotten it "a long time ago at a Christmas party," and then launched into the story of her personal reality. When I realized what was happening, I frantically groped around for my notebook, because, naturally, the tape recorder was not in sight. The following excerpt is from my written record of Jiana's narrative, together with the children's responses.

JIANA: My father was on stage talking to his friends, and he did it, he was in this program. My father doing it . . . did something bad, and he's in a program, and I can't tell you why . . . . It's something white . . . . It starts with a C, but I don't want to tell. And it's called . . . . . . cocaine . . . . . And that's why he's in the program, and he'll never come out.

ROBIN: What do you mean by what you said, your father's doing it? I don't understand.

JIANA: It's like something bad, like mommy goes in a closet and I say, "what are you doing?" She says, "You don't need to know," and she's sneaking a cigarette. And I say, that's not good for you. My father sometimes . .- . . . . . Sometimes if he says he's coming to pick you up . . . and he doesn't come . . . . . . don't say he's a liar, say he's a fibber.

In essence, Jiana had used the prop of the Christmas ball to enable her finally to launch into the story she really wanted to tell. She had been guarded at first, but then seemed to decide to explain everything, and in doing so finally established a context for her presence in our class. I felt at the time that this was one of those situations that sneak up on you and create a huge dilemma. Although in my role as a member of the audience I would never stop the discussion, I was worried that this kind of talk was not appropriate for the classroom. It was similar to hearing the most secret of family secrets. But I also realized that Jiana had waited four months to share this, and she knew, I think, that we could receive this information and that it would be important to us.

ANDY: What does "cocaine" mean?

JIANA: That means like drugs and stuff.

ANDY: You mean your father used drugs?

JIANA: No. My father took drugs . . . . . and my mother kicked him out and he went in a program.

CINDY: What's a program?

JIANA: It means that when a lot of people have problems when he got kicked out he went to a program.

ROBIN: What's a program? I don't understand.

JIANA: A program means you don't have no place to live, and you, you just stay there for awhile and when you you're ready to go find a house, you go find a house.

The children listened carefully to her explanations, and there was a feeling of extreme seriousness in the group. They wanted to understand and questioned her closely about meanings of words. They empathized and gave support, and as the discussion expanded I was not uncomfortable because Jiana was very composed. She was not ashamed. She was just telling her story, and a look at her language shows how well constructed and coherent her story is, how layered her reality. Note in the text, how her talk has changed. There are no *um*'s and *uh*'s, fewer long pauses, no crutches. This is real talk. This is powerful talk. A question lingered, however: Was this appropriate for school? Should a child be allowed publicly to disclose to her classmates the difficult circumstances of her life? As I listened, I knew that to stop the conversation would have been akin to censoring her world. My decision to let her continue reflected, I think, my intuition that this child's wish to tell her story took precedence over my discomfort at hearing it.

THE BEGINNING OF FAKE STORIES

In late February, I decided to declare March a month of sharing without objects. The sessions had become formulaic, or so I perceived, and I wanted to refresh the process. Some children grumbled that there would not be anything to share, but for Jiana this did not pose new problems because she had few objects to share. In the second week in March, following a child's account of a trip to a zoo, Jiana got in the chair and launched into a narrative about how she went to the zoo with her mother and the zookeeper came out and took the gorillas out on a leash for her mother to pet. This was simply too much for me, and I blurted out, "Jiana, this is a time for true stories!" But she was adamant that the event had occurred and tried to continue her story.

No sooner were the words out of my mouth than all the children in the group turned around and looked at me very hard and long. Time seemed to stop for me as I realized from the change in their expressions what I had done. They turned slowly back, mumbling about it's not being true, how it could not be true. Jiana tried to maintain her story in the face of their questions about how a gorilla would come out. She shifted to say maybe she just saw the gorillas outside in their play area, then asked quickly for questions and comments. A few kind children tried to fix the story: "Maybe it was chimpanzees" and "maybe it was a petting zoo," but within those few seconds her audience had turned away from her. Afterwards I spoke with Jiana, trying to explain my actions, and really, I thought to myself, my betrayal. I was the one person who had always supported her in the chair.

She admitted to me that you could not really pet a gorilla. I asked her if she could come in the next day and tell a real, true story, and she agreed, but I still felt sick about my own behavior. The next day Jiana did not come to school. Sarah got up and shared a story about a swimming incident in which her sister fell out of a boat and swam with the dolphins. The story was obviously a complete fabrication, and a few children said, "That can't be true!" and turned again to ask me, "Is that true?" But this time I did not respond. During the questions and comments the children cross-examined Sarah on the issue of truth and realism, refuting her story line. Sarah tried to maintain the story but got caught in inconsistent details. I asked myself what was going on. Was the power of the chair so great that it made you do anything to stay in it? Did some children secretly admire Jiana's story and wish to emulate it? More importantly, I wondered why I had defined the sharing narrative to mean true stories. Clearly, I was lagging behind some of these 6- and 7-year-olds in my conceptualization of what sharing time was.

That was how our exploration of "fake" stories began. The next day, I apologized to the children and to Jiana for my behavior and told them that it seemed as if we needed to expand our format. April would be a month in which children could tell true or fake stories. (The children and I called the stories "fake stories" to distinguish them from first-person accounts of real events, although at the time I was not comfortable with the use of the word *fake*. It seemed, however, to be a term all the children could identify.) Again, as with the switch to sharing without objects, there was some grumbling among the group. Many children said they did not know how to tell fake stories.

Jiana continued to share true stories, and she was gaining in fluency and responsiveness to her audience, often using their comments as an opportunity to amplify her narrative — a technique she had seen used skillfully by others. In early April, after a week in which no child chose to make up a story, Robin sat in the chair and made an attempt. She told about a trip to a beach where she found "diamond shells." The children asked many questions, and she made up more as she responded. There were no comments, so I volunteered an improvised comment about how I flew my plane to Florida yesterday. Robin got out of the chair, and Duncan took her place. He also told a story about a make-believe trip and asked for questions or comments. Jiana raised her hand, and her comment follows:

> When I went to Mars, . . it was pouring and it was freezing, . . . and
> I was shivering, and we put the heater on, and I was hot. When
> Karen came, it started to snow, and it floated up the whole world.
> She asked if she could come in my house. Then all the water came
> up, and all the clothes were soaking.

The other children were hysterical with laughter; they had been taken completely by surprise. They howled and hushed each other as she talked so they could hear. Jiana's comment was followed by five others, and most of those were modeled on hers.

After sharing, we moved to writing, and, for the first time that year, Jiana said she had an idea for writing a book. She wanted to write about her trip to Mars. I realized that it would be important for her not to labor over the writing of the book. Since she still was not able to write using invented spelling and had few sight words to call upon, I asked her to draw first. She was very purposeful and immediately drew her most well developed pictures of the school year. They were clear, and she had a text ready to dictate. It occurred to me, as she spoke and then read without hesitation the text I had written, that I had wasted six months trying to have Jiana work in a writing format that worked for most first graders — a brief prewriting conference about their ideas — but not for Jiana. Something in the process of forming this oral narrative had made it possible for her to "write," or at least to represent a complete text. The sharing experience enabled me to see that if Jiana was going to write stories, she must first tell them as a public text. How many other children, I wondered, might do better with the same approach?

Two days later, Jiana told her first full-blown fantasy story. In it she described how she and I had climbed a tree, and she developed the story to include every child and adult in the class. The story was very repetitive in that as she added a new child to the tree, she would recite the names, in order, of every child who had gone before, and it also included many transformations. For example:

> Then Karen turned into a monkey, and she said "Quack, quack."
> Then Karen K. [student teacher] turned into a monkey, and she said, "Quack, quack." Then Franny came along and ate them, and ate all the kids, and Franny threw up, and all little spiders came out, and Kenshi came and ate all the spiders.

She told her story for 15 minutes, and the children were beside themselves with delight. Their laughter literally echoed throughout the primary unit.

In telling this story, Jiana used a number of dramatic techniques she had not used before. She had a much broader range of movement. Instead of perching on the edge of the chair, she sat back in it as if she owned it, with her hand on her hip, leaning back and forth over the children, gesturing and pointing to different members of the audience. When the laughter became too hilarious, she would say, as she leaned over shaking her finger, "Shhh! Are you listening?", and they would quiet. She used different inflections for the voices of different children, and the story was very fluid, changing pace as she paused to see who she had forgotten, and then picking up momentum as she decided their actions.

This was the first time Jiana had been fully herself in the chair. She had spent the year figuring out how to talk in sharing and then had adapted the model to her own style. Once she had become fully acclimated to school, she was then able to influence our level of discourse so that she could fully participate.

Jiana continued to tell fantasy stories. At some points, she was not prepared for her turn to share and would ask someone else to go while she thought. I would hear her next to me, trying to say the opening sentences of her story. When she had them straight, she would get in the chair and begin. Her stories were always accompanied by raucous laughter and great audience involvement by most of the children. After awhile, though, I noticed the reactions of some of my Caucasian boys to Jiana's narratives. For several weeks, none of them had seemed able to participate in her stories. They were clearly uncomfortable with both the completely different styles of the stories and with the responses of their classmates. They would often say to one another, "This doesn't make any sense."

One day, as I was observing their reactions very closely, I noticed their discomfort as she began. They looked at one another, began private conversations, and two in the front row turned their bodies away from her as she spoke. Joel said to the children around him, who were laughing at the narrative, "This isn't funny," and he lay down on the floor. The other boys looked bored and very severe. As Jiana went on, she built a series of sequential stories using different children in the class, which was a format she had established and which was being used by other children for their stories. She was always very careful not to include these boys because they had objected very strongly to being involved in the stories. Each time she shared, Jiana would check with them saying, for example, "Donald, do you want to be in it?" Normally, they would refuse. As I watched, the boys gradually relaxed as the uproar gained momentum and Jiana tried to calm the class by naming more children to be included. By the time she was finished, they were smiling, and laughing. By the third week, they, too, were encouraging Jiana to tell fake stories and would allow her to use their names.

A NEW GENRE IS BORN

What the boys perceived early on, and later came to accept, was that Jiana was changing the rules for storytelling in our class. That kind of change signaled, I think, that Jiana had some sort of special authority when she was in the chair, that she could put words and ideas together in ways that were unfamiliar and even provocative, that she had an ability to use language in a way that was difficult for these very articulate and privileged boys to understand. But the genre that she was developing was so compelling and inclusive that, in the end, even they could not resist participating in her stories.

The fictional stories became more frequent. Every child in the class began to include them in their repertoires. Several expanded the format to include call-and-response sequences in which their language became repetitive, much like a predictable storybook, and they allowed their audience to take over the repeating part of the text. Jiana began to introduce new uses of different elements from the children's daily lives. For example, she adapted her voice to use their speaking patterns and included current events in the class, such as Joel's chicken pox. Her stories continued to be inclusive narratives in which every child in the class was named and included as a central character at some point. To her, the entire class belonged in her story.

JIANA: When I went to Mars um, Karen and Karen K. um, they had little pieces of hair sticking up . (*laughter*) and um, and Karen uh, Karen (*whispers to me, pointing to the rosebud necklace I am wearing,*

"what are those?" I answer "roses . . . rosebuds, rosebuds") and when
Karen had the rosebuds on she had her little kid with her . . .

OTHERS: She doesn't have one!

JIANA: And it was Robin

OTHERS: Ahhhhhh

JIANA: and um, . . . No! And his boy, her boy was Robin's boyfriend was
um, uh, let's see. I'm not gonna pick Andy because he doesn't like it.
Awww. Oh no . . . Manon. No, Bridget? No, wait, who?

OTHERS: You! Manon!

JIANA: Manon. So when Manon went out with Karen, 'cause that's her
mother, and, Manon's my sister . . . . Me and Manon went out and
saw Andy. Manon said (*speaking in a high voice*) "Andy, um, um,
will you come over to my house to have dinner?" I said (*in her own
voice*) "um, ssshhh, ask him if he wants to go out to the restaurant!"
And so she said, "Oh, um, um (*high voice again*)

OTHERS: Eeewwww. Yuck!

JIANA: Can we go to the restaurant? Can we go out to the restaurant?
And he said (*loudly*), "NO!" And so she said, "I never can get a
boyfriend." And so she asked Joel. (*loud laughter*)

JOEL: No!

JIANA: And so Joel said, "Yesss."

JOEL: No, No!

JIANA: Joel, Joel said, "NO!" So she asked William.

OTHERS: Oooohhhh!

WILLIAM: And I said, "No."

JIANA: And he said, "No."

The domino effect continued. Children incorporated Jiana's initiatives, using immediate context to tell their stories, such as including what
other children were wearing or holding in their hands at meeting, using
naturalistic dialogue between characters, expanding their body language
to augment the story and manage the audience, transforming their settings
in time and place, and, finally, even using her model of inclusive stories
to insert themselves into friendships within the class that they wished they
had. Duncan, for example, who had been ignored by the boys' circle for
the entire year and did not appear to know how to initiate friendships,
began to develop stories in which he and the boys spent time together. He
was able to get their attention and support by semantically placing himself
within their group and by developing the characters in his stories around
each boy's particular interests. I noticed in early June that all of the boys
had begun to include Duncan in their play and that they finally viewed
him as a friend.

What was most remarkable, however, was the way Jiana's initiative enabled so many children to engage in a new way of talking. Of course, this did not occur without struggle for some very competent talkers. William, for example, who had quite a high level of mastery over mainstream narrative style, absolutely would not make any attempt at the fantasy format. I literally had to force him to try it by refusing to let him share some x-rays of his brother's broken arm until he told us a fake story. After I realized how different and challenging the fictional narratives were, I asked every child to try at least one fake story before they returned to a showing format.

When William saw that I was serious, he got in the chair but could not speak (from fear I think) and was literally fighting back tears. He struggled for several seconds to compose himself and finally started to talk, but very softly with his head turned away from the audience.

> One day I went to Joel's house to play, and we built a spaceship. We wanted to go to Jupiter, but Joel's mom wouldn't let us. So we decided to sneak.

As he talked, he continued to look aside. Shelly asked him to speak louder, and I repeated the request. He continued, and the children began to titter. His eyes brightened, and he became caught up in the story, turning his shoulders towards the children. Then, with a gleam in his eyes and a smile on his face, he said,

> so Joel's mom went looking for us in the closet, and she fell into a box and got stuck.

The children loved that idea, and with their reaction he completely relaxed, made eye contact with his audience, and told a long story about the trip: how they got to where the aliens were,

> and they said, "Who are you?," and we said, "We're from earth," and they said, "You're aliens," and we said, "No, you're aliens." I guess we were all aliens.

and then concluded that they "returned through the maze of the black hole" to find Joel's mother still in the box. The story lasted 10 minutes, and when he was finished, he was radiant.

In the same way that William was challenged, Andy, an African-American child, found his public voice through the use of fantasy stories. Andy had not really participated in sharing throughout the year. Like

Jiana, he seemed to have very few material things that he wanted to share. He would usually sit in the back during sharing, muttering to himself (a behavior I had observed in his brother the prior year). However, he was always a very active questioner and commenter, seeming to take pleasure in participating in the sharing but resisting any central role. In late April, however, Andy tried his first story. It was basically a remake of the three little pigs, using, instead, three little rabbits, and he was very self-conscious. He included other children, but only his friends. Two weeks later he had become a regular sharer, and by early June he was asking to get up and share every day. Clearly, he had found his form.

His later stories were very inclusive and broke the mold, which his friends had established, of excluding girls. In Andy's stories the girls and boys were equally matched both in importance and in power. One day in late May, after telling a fabulously long and complicated story about Joel and the girls that had great detail about different settings, Andy and Sarah (who had also shared before him) asked if they could continue their stories later in the day at our activity time. They both asked those children who wanted to hear the rest of their story to raise their hands. Then they instructed those children to remember who they were so that when they called them back, they would know to come and listen. Sure enough, about 45 minutes later I looked up to see six or seven children gathering on the steps at their feet to hear the rest of their stories. The children built block towers as they listened, and the scene was so natural that I knew something important had happened. The power of the stories, and the community of listeners that the stories created, had become a part of the fabric of our classroom.

But by that time, Jiana had vanished. Her frequent absences, which began in winter, had multiplied, and soon she disappeared: phone disconnected, address unknown. She was dropped as a case by the social worker because her family could not be found.

ANALYSIS

What, then, is the value of sharing time in the primary classroom? An analysis of how this teacher research drastically changed classroom contexts for the teaching of language must be located within my own attempts to understand the evolution of this sharing process. Most particularly, to appreciate the importance of Jiana's contribution to the children's language, I must locate her narrative style in the context of school language. Certainly in most schools, fake narratives, as we came to call them, are not central to the children's study of oral language. However, it became clear as Jiana initiated her narrative style, and then as other children struggled to work with her genre, that a different sort of thinking and talking, one that many competent talkers had not encountered, was going on.

Mikkelsen (1990) outlines the literary modes used by black children in storymaking narratives: retelling, borrowing, re-creation, blending, and transformation. Jiana's infusion of fantasy stories into our sharing introduced all of these elements as narrative tools. These were not devices that most of the children were comfortable using in their narratives, but virtually all of the children made attempts to incorporate them into their talk, and they continued to work on these skills long after Jiana had left us. Mikkelsen's notion of storymaking as a "third literacy, a way we 'read' ourselves into understanding of the world, as well as a way to 'write' a new version of the world we are trying to see" (1990, p. 13), was also very evident as the children's narratives evolved.

The new narratives became vehicles for sorting out, most particularly, the separation between boys and girls and for pulling this class of children together through their fictional play. Jiana began that process by telling inclusionary, "sociocentric" stories, but her classmates went along with her, continuously attempting to consolidate their social world by developing a fictional life in which every child and every adult were playmates.

The body of stories that grew from Jiana's initiatives expanded the children's collective folklore to include forays into fantasy. As Paley (1990) says, "the classroom that does not create its own legends has not traveled beneath the surface to where the living takes place" (p. 5). Certainly the true stories had created a rich historical background that constantly supported and expanded our development as a community. We had a growing body of common experiences and shared accounts that we could repeatedly refer to in our interactions: in essence a semantic history that distinguished our community from all others and made our speech more sociocentric. Only we, as a first-grade class, had access to certain discussions.

The fictional stories, however, expanded the children's ability to speak about the more subterranean issues of the community: about belonging and exclusion, about unspoken wishes to overcome barriers to a cohesive membership. Duncan wished to be a friend, and Andy searched for his public voice. Every child added a new level of understanding and articulation to their narratives, and relationships did change.

Paley's vision of the storyteller as a "culture builder" who depends on audience participation to build a new group reality is clear in the excerpt from Jiana's Rosebud Story, where she actively constructed her image of the group by responding to the audience remarks and interruptions. In this storytelling genre, interruptions by the audience give the teller cues as to what the community of listeners wants (needs?) to have happen. Clarifying the relationship between storytelling and the development of classroom culture gives the genre Jiana introduced added power and importance. Hers is not a private, egocentric vision of her world; it is a vision that puts forth her sense that everyone belongs, and attempts, also, to respect each person's point of view. It is a vision that in the end was important for all the children and for me as well.

And so Jiana enabled us all to move out into new levels of expression and communal life, but similarly, with the help of her friends Jiana also gained some fluency in mainstream narratives that would not have developed had my stance as her teacher been different. My role as a teacher-researcher intervened to Jiana's benefit in two ways. First, I was not at the center of the sharing dyad. Had I been, what I originally viewed as the impoverishment of her language would have been too glaring to ignore. As Bernstein (1972) says, "if the teacher has to say continuously, 'Say it again, darling, I didn't understand you', then in the end the child may say nothing" (p. 149). I would have felt compelled to coach Jiana in mainstream language or to refer her for special help. In any case, my actions would have identified her as being in some way inadequate. Second, by recording and reflecting on the changes in our sharing process, I was continuously forced to reevaluate my preconception of what sharing time was. The reflective stance compelled me to think critically about the children's points of view and about my own limitations as a listener.

Bakhtin's description (1986) of the ways in which speaker and listener interact helps to clarify how Jiana's language and ours became more congruent. He points out that in each utterance "we embrace, understand, and sense the speaker's speech plan or speech will" (p. 77). In doing so we are able to understand the speaker's intent and measure when the speaker is through. However, with Jiana — and, I would venture, with many children who do not understand mainstream classroom discourse — the children and I were initially not able to understand her speech plan. She could not mark it in the appropriate ways so that we could follow her. Apparently she had never been in a setting where she had learned to use school discourse, but remarkably, after study and what appeared to be many unsuccessful attempts, she could understand the structure sufficiently to master it in a very short period of time and then transform it in a way that took other children to new and different levels of talk. How did this happen?

Perhaps in Bakhtin's (1981) conceptualization of "heteroglossia" one can build an answer. Because Bakhtin views languages as interactive, the social aspect of producing language moves to the forefront as a powerful force in forming, and ultimately in transforming, a particular discourse. This viewpoint helps elucidate the transformations that Jiana and the other children went through. Jiana brought a discourse to school that did not fit the mainstream. But in the interaction of two worlds of communication, new forms were created, new forms of speech as well as of response. As the children observed me privileging Jiana's attempts by my silent support and as they took on the role of ratifying her speech, their ethic of social inclusion, rather than school notions of inclusion, took control of their responses. They, as social beings, desired to respond to Jiana because she was clearly a full member of our group.

In the same way, Jiana's strong desire to master the sharing discourse was completely bound up with her desire to become part of our community. Her struggle to understand the intention of the sharing narrative illustrates what Bakhtin (1981) calls the "socially charged life" of the world (p. 293). This was her impetus. In the same way, the other children in the class, in trying to understand her speech plan, further pulled her into the discourse, making it easier for her to appropriate their language forms to her purposes. They made clear how the language could serve her; they were explicit in their tutoring.

Hence, to understand the transformation of Jiana's language, we begin and end with her place in the community of the classroom. Had I chosen to isolate Jiana as a speaker early in the year by referring her immediately for outside help, I would have prevented her from acquiring a new and difficult discourse. More importantly, the dynamic of new language acquisition that I observed over the course of the year on so many different levels would never have happened, and we would have been the poorer for it. Clearly Jiana had a tremendous impact on the life of this classroom, and as I observed and reflected on the process of sharing, my ability to understand Jiana's language, and in fact the language of all the children, deepened. As the children enabled her to understand a new and important way of talking and as I labored to understand their actions, so Jiana enabled all of us to expand our understanding and practice of a new genre.

When she was in school, Jiana was completely present and focused on communicating. She always attempted to participate in even the most difficult kinds of exchanges, and although she did not have time to consolidate many of her skills, she learned how to use every bit of her life experience to enable her to join the other children in many different ways of talking. I now believe that most, if not all, children, each in their own way, have the same purpose when in school. Because Jiana was a respected member of the community, the other children tried to respond to all her attempts at communication, both successful and unsuccessful. I have learned that when each member of the classroom community strives to affirm the importance of all voices, the benefit for every child is much greater. If children like Jiana could only be held on to, embraced rather than isolated in the life of the classroom, they would prove themselves to be more than capable of participating in, and enriching, every aspect of classroom life.

3

Making Room for Many Voices

This is the story of an immigrant child who came to my classroom as most immigrant children do, new to the country and uninitiated into the cultural conventions that drive schooling in the United States. She presented the problems for me that many immigrant children bring with them: problems of language, of cultural difference, of educational disadvantage. What is represented in her story, however, is the tremendous complexity of gaining entrance into this culture and the overwhelming isolation these children must endure, an isolation imposed by immersion in an unfamiliar language and culture and by the sudden imposition of silence. For these children, their own language becomes dysfunctional, and communication about their most basic needs and wishes is submerged.

Classroom teachers who are confronted with immigrant children are also faced with this wall of silence. We are often unable to speak the child's language and know little of his or her native culture. Thus the process of teaching and enculturating an immigrant child into the classroom sometimes becomes an exercise in false starts, faux pas, and frustration. In many cases, we are compelled to teach the most basic kinds of language skills, a kind of language teaching we are unprepared to do. In contrast to this, these children must be included in mainstream classroom events, many of which reflect more difficult curricular goals and instructional activities. When my class of 20-odd children studies science, we all must study science, including Nobuyuki, who spends most lessons rocking back and forth and creating his own white noise to drown out the din of English, or Shin, who turns his back on me as I attempt to teach, or Mami, so frail and passive that my attempts to lead her to a table are met with a limp hand and an impenetrable silence.

Jiana had helped me to begin to understand how a shared class history is built that then allows even the most disadvantaged children to engage fully in the act of learning as a community. As I followed Jiana through the year, I came to see the importance of paying attention to the most mundane of classroom events and of living in the classroom, as it were, a closely examined life. In the process of documenting sharing time for that year, I also began to think carefully about other children who were attempting, from positions of great disadvantage, to participate in the process. At times, the most compelling participants were children new to this country who, working against extreme barriers to communication, developed strategies for sharing their lives with us. Many times, without speaking, they would sit in the sharing chair and provoke long interactions with other children and myself, interactions that in some cases they could barely join. In effect, they were the centerpiece of a class's attempt to be inclusive and welcoming, sitting in the chair as symbols of the extremity to which that labor sometimes must go.

How can a teacher make room for the many voices a classroom must assimilate when some of the voices are not even speaking the same language? I believe that that process of assimilation begins with the interaction of teacher and child, and then teacher, child, and classmates as they search for common ground from which to build a shared language and a new history. That these children are difficult to include does not free us from an obligation to do so; it simply adds another layer of difficulty to the already complex process of teaching. However, the process of looking for meanings in, and clues to the stories of immigrant children, and of building a framework for inclusion, began for me, in contrast to Jiana's story, with a record of their simple interactions and forays into the life of the classroom. Language records alone could not suffice.

As a teacher-researcher thinking about the needs of children from other cultures, my use of data has to expand to include a more semiotic orientation. In other words, any artifact I can gather, most especially those signs or symbols that have meanings independent of spoken language, might help me construct the "planks in a bridge from one culture to another" (Ashton-Warner, 1963, p. 31) that will further expand our social community. Thus the process of collecting the minutiae of classroom interactions and events: records of small conversations or interactions, drawings, discarded notes, doodles, and observations take on new importance. These documents enable me to see through the barriers of silence and cultural difference and to pull the child into the classroom culture. Thus the story of Imani and her entry into my classroom unfolded as I documented her development using as many sources as I could discover.

IMANI'S STORY

On a cold January morning, Imani entered school, newly arrived from a small country in Africa. Seven years old and registered in first grade, she wore her hair carefully braided in a basket design and was wearing a pink snow hat that she would not remove. Imani had obviously never seen a place like this before. In meeting, early on in that first morning, she was plastered against the wall, her face a mask: no smile, no response, no panic or fear, none of the tears that often accompany a sudden entry into a new school in a new country — just silence.

After meeting I interviewed Imani, asking about her country and her school. She told me a story in an accented English that I could barely understand. I thought it sounded more Creole than English, and I checked her registration card. It said she spoke English. I guessed that was a matter of interpretation, but the gist of her story as far as I could tell was that she had never been to school before. She pulled out her backpack and proudly showed me a brand new book that her mother had just bought her. She said she had never had a book before. After several tries, I was able to understand that statement. Out of the backpack came crayons and a pack of markers, also her first. Then Imani told me that she had just met her mother — at least that's what I thought she said. I realized I had better go on a search for more information.

In speaking to the staff members who did the intake interview, I was able to piece together some of Imani's history. It was the kind of account I had read about in newspapers but never experienced first hand. Apparently, after her birth, Imani's mother became quite ill and was sent to the United States, where she had a relative and could receive the medical care she needed. Imani, an infant, was left with her two siblings in the care of a large extended family. After her mother recovered, she was unable to return to her country for reasons involving money as well as the fact that a civil war had broken out, making it dangerous to return. After seven years of separation, she and Imani had just met.

As I watched Imani, I wondered how to help her. She was, from my point of view as a teacher of early readers, completely illiterate and without the conventional resources that even the most delayed children bring to school. She had never been to school, owned books, drawn with markers, painted, or used simple educational materials. It struck me that Imani had had less access to the materials that begin a child's journey toward literacy than many of this country's poorest children. By the end of her first day in school, though, she was acting like a healthy, intelligent child. The girls in the class had taken her under their wing, managing to get her through the lunch line and playing with her at recess. She was smiling and fooling around a little, but she was completely ignorant of school protocols such as lining up, using books, and drawing. She did, however, seem to be very good at making friends.

Over the next few days the language problem grew. Imani was listed as an English speaker. So was I, of course. However, I could not understand her and she could not understand me. When she talked to me I felt helpless and frustrated. She was very willing to do what I said, when she understood me, but she had no background in school. I began to keep notes of what she could and could not do. On her fifth day in school, I noted in my journal:

> Imani learns to do these things: line up, stand in the line, follow the line to its destination, and listen to a tape of a book and turn the pages at the signal. After one run through with the story of *The Little Red Hen*, Imani has the format down. She listens to the book five times in a row, each time reciting along with the tape very loudly in her own dialect and looking at the pictures. That cracks everybody up.

By her fifth day in school, Imani's art journal pictures showed a remarkable development, akin to seeing the developmental milestones of art in fast forward. From the first page of the journal, where she had drawn minute line drawings of undistinguishable figures, painstakingly and lovingly trying to use the markers (Figure 3.1), Imani rapidly progressed to full-page drawings of children and houses that showed African characteristics and style of expression (Figure 3.2). On the Monday of her second week in school, I noted the following conversation, which occurred while Imani was painting for the first time:

> "Karen," she calls out, as she stands in front of the easel and a half-finished picture. "I need green!" "Mix it," I call back. "How to mix it?" she returns. "With the other colors." "Other colors?" she says to herself. I walk down to the art area, get her a tray, and show her how to mix different color paints on the tray, then return to the table where I am working. She takes a brush and begins mixing paint. Thirty seconds later I hear, "Karen, look! It's green!", and so it is. Imani paints a room with furniture, a chair and a table. The chair is green and painted three dimensionally. (Figure 3.3)

In meeting, Imani began to take great delight in raising her hand and trying to say something even when she did not have a clue as to what we were talking about. She seemed to relish the mannerisms and rituals of school and the audience that the children in the classroom provided. Although we could not seem to communicate about her life in Africa, she would try to explain her drawings. In her picture story book, she drew typical 6-year-old pictures: house, candy, sun, taking pleasure in reading those words slowly and loudly from her sight-word cards. Then one day,

Figure 3.1. Imani's first drawing.

after drawing a picture of a man and asking for the word *dad*, she told me her father did not come to America. When I asked why, she recounted a story of drunkenness and abuse. The children sitting with us at the table were silent, but their ears were like elephants' as they strained to understand her, somehow inferring from her tone and seriousness the deeper message she was presenting. Across the table from her, Sam's eyes grew huge and sad. He was completely still. I could see the "truth" of this story seeping in (truth being a serious preoccupation of Sam's). He always asked for the truth or nontruth of the stories he heard, and Imani had laid a child's true story in his lap.

Imani realized quickly that books were a major preoccupation of our classroom, and she labored to master their use. She soon learned basic reading protocols: left to right progression, pointing to the text as it was

Figure 3.2. Imani's drawings two weeks later.

read, and looking at the pictures for clues as to what the story was about. However, the behavioral expectations, the language demands, and the pace of the classroom tried her patience. In our class meetings she was inattentive and sullen, often burying her head in her arms at sharing time and silently teasing other children. I quickly learned that Imani could be quite stubborn if corrected. She did not exactly refuse to do things, she just did not move from where she was, staring at me with an impassive face and a steely, motionless body. I became unsure about what I was seeing: Was it a deepening anger at being thrust into a new country with a new language, something I had seen frequently in immigrant children. Or was it a cultural response to my authority? I could tell that I was not addressing her in the right way to elicit a response. I decided that I needed help.

Figure 3.3. Imani's first painting.

In early February, as I continued to search for more information on Imani's country of origin, culture, and dialect, she began to try new things. She wrote her first entry at writing time, began to put notes in our mailbox, and announced to me that she was going to share. Her art journal showed a new focus on presenting images that represented a complete idea.

One morning she drew a girl eating a banana and looking up at a star. The star was round and had stripes of color like a rainbow (Figure 3.4). When I questioned Imani about the picture, I realized that the image of a star as a round, glowing orb was free of the stereotypic five-pointed rendering of our culture. Imani was presenting me with a clean, unencumbered picture of how a culturally uninitiated child thought about the world and about school, unencumbered in that her image was not bounded by a culturally determined form of representation. Thus the image told more about her perception and incipient understanding of the stars she had observed in the night sky in Africa than a more rigid symbol ever could. I began to see that she was teaching me about adaptation and intelligence in a very different way from most of my students. The process of observing her and collecting data became more precious.

But new initiatives to teach Imani seemed to frustrate her. In every

Figure 3.4. Imani's image of a girl looking at a star.

situation, she resisted any teacher direction or control, crossing her arms, turning her head to the side, or covering her ears and staring off into space. Teaching Imani was a monumental task, requiring intense negotiations that, in late February, out of frustration, I decided to abandon. I sat down to work with her one morning, and she refused to join me, leaning like lead against the wall with crossed arms and staring at me like a sphinx. I pulled out a chair and pointed to it, urging her in. She sat finally, arms still folded across her chest, staring straight ahead. When she refused to help me "read" an old text from her picture story book, I decided to invoke reality and gave her a lecture, using a picture because I was not sure how much she would understand. I drew Imani in relation to the rest of the class:

Imani ————————————————⟶ class

I explained to her that she had come in late to our class, and I directed her to look around the room at the other children, who were hard at work on their reading.

"This is like a race," I said. "We are here, running fast, working hard, and you are here. To catch up, you will have to run faster and work harder."

She fixed me with an impassive stare and then slowly turned her body away. So I continued, "I can't teach you if you don't want to learn. So when you're ready to learn, call me." And I walked away and sat down with another child on the other side of the classroom, leaving her with her face in her arms. Thirty seconds later, just as I began to feel a tinge of remorse for the tone of my remarks, I heard a voice, soft and African, like a song. "Karen, I'm ready."

JOINING THE CLASSROOM COMMUNITY

The other children were also having the same problem with Imani. When confronted with her as a resisting member of their small learning groups, they would take a deep breath and give me a dirty look. Yet they were somehow more persuasive than I. In movement one day, Tom, who was leading her small group, handled her masterfully. When she did not respond or move at his request, he got up, took her hand and brought her over, showing what he wanted her to do. She did it with no resistance. I was clearly at a disadvantage. Some children, however, particularly girls, soon tired of Imani's fierce pride. At recess one afternoon, Imani walked up to me and said, "Karen, I have to report Michelle, Manon, and Bobbi."

"Why?" I asked.

"Because when I ask if they will play with me, they say, 'No!'"

Michelle, Manon, and Bobbi were busy swinging on the monkey bars, and I went over to discuss the charge with them. They admitted it was true, but insisted that Imani never wanted to play their way. (I knew that that was probably true, too.) However, I pled Imani's case, reminding Manon and Michelle, both of whom had been new immigrants last year, how hard it was to be new to this country and trying to make friends. The girls were remorseful and said they would make up with Imani. Thus began a serious friendship, as they took Imani under their wing and began to teach her how to do many things: how to use the monkey bars, how to listen to a story, how to do her work.

As the children took Imani in, I found that my job was easier. I also found that I had a definite fascination with Imani's dialect, having spoken a form of pidgin English myself as a child. Hearing Imani speak reminded me of my early childhood language. In private conversations with her, I found myself speaking more and more like Imani and less and less like my adult self. Finally, in March, I found out more details of Imani's culture and, more importantly for our communication problems, her dialect, and made these notes in my journal:

IMANI'S DIALECT

1. Has no negatives. Negative is denoted by stress.
   I *can* do it. (I can't do it.)
   I can *do* it. (I can do it.)
2. Has no final consonants.
   book = buh
   girl = gih
3. There are no plurals.
   girls = gih
   girl = gih

   books = buh
   book = buh
(Although these clues help me to talk to Imani, I realize the problem they will present with phonics instruction.) *yes*

The communication gap began to narrow, and the children also started to understand her better.

In April, much as Jiana began to use the sharing format to tell her stories, Imani became a regular sharer, first sharing a Barbie doll she had just received, then a bracelet and rings her mother had given her. In mid-March, she told a nursery rhyme, Jack and Jill, reciting it in a song. She was embarrassed and hid her face as she sang. In the questions and comments, Sheri noted that she couldn't hear her and asked her if she would do it again. The other children agreed loudly and asked to hear it again. Imani smiled and laughed and said she would sing it again. All at once the children in the audience moved forward as one body, like a wave, until they were crowded around her, almost on top of her. Imani was overwhelmed and hid her face again, then decided to sing. The children applauded when she was done. The next week she told a story "that I heard in Africa," much of which was unintelligible but very melodious. That story also contained a repeating song, and the children asked her to sing the song more than once. Then a week later, she told an improv-

isational story about friendship, using her characteristically slow and
thoughtful pace. It was a story about "Michelle, Manon, and Bobbi, and
what children think when their friends won't play with them." In this
story, the girls would not play with Andy. It was also a story about Michelle's imagination. In the story, Michelle:

> *As I transcribed it*: wan to flĭ. Bŭ she dĭ naw no haw. She loo
>   ŭ, an she see a būtifu gō haw ŭ
>   ĭ dey skĭ, an a sunsĕ shĭn ovah dey haw.

> *In translation*: (wanted to fly. But she did not know how. She looked
> up, and she sees a beautiful gold house up in the sky, and a sunset
> shining over the house.)

The language was languid and richly toned, delivered in Imani's melodious style. Tom, sitting next to me, with his characteristic love of words
was translating to himself as he listened, sometimes saying to me, "Did
she say _____ ?" to check and see if he was right. It was late in the day,
and some of the children seemed restless. I wondered if they were bored,
but in the questions and comments that followed it was apparent that
they had listened and understood. Tom commented that she was a good
storyteller. Our expert in facile language obviously was beginning to appreciate the cadence and tone of Imani's style of storytelling.

As Imani became more engaged in being taught, I began to assume
that her new motivation meant that her level of comprehension of the
curriculum I taught was also increasing. Like many children who appear
to be bilingual, however, her grasp of our dialect was only superficially
improved. In May, after reading a book on reptiles that offered a very
clear discussion of reptiles and what distinguished them from mammals,
fish, and birds, Imani raised her hand and asked, "What is a reptile?" She
was still back at the title of the book. I was shocked and groped for a response which would hide my annoyance.

"Do you mean, what does the word *reptile* mean, or what is the word
for?" I asked, trying to distinguish between whether she was misunderstanding a description of an animal or a semantic category (classes of
animals). Michelle tried to explain the idea over again to her, but Imani
still did not understand.

"I don't understand," she said, patiently. "What do you mean, 'reptile'?"

I was stumped. As the weeks went on, and Imani became more interested in learning, our miscommunications became more obvious. Perhaps

it was that Imani was now able to ask the questions she had had all along, or that she had learned enough of our dialect to communicate about content, or perhaps it was that she was simply paying more attention to the curriculum because she finally understood the exchange between teacher and child that the teaching/learning process embodied. Either way, she presented me with increasingly more puzzling questions.

In June, as the butterflies hatched out of their chrysalises, Imani was looking intently into the butterfly box. She was captivated with the beautiful colors of the newly emerged butterflies, which were resting on some flowers inside the box. I wondered whether Imani understood the science of what we were doing. In other words, when watching the process of metamorphosis, had she connected caterpillar to chrysalis to butterfly? Somehow I had always assumed that seeing it in front of you day by day should do the trick. I asked her, "Where do the butterflies come from?" She looked at me blankly and waited for me to try again. "Can you tell me how the butterflies grew in here?" Still blank, and waiting, she made no response. "Where do you think they came from?" and I pointed into the box, which had the empty chrysalis hanging on the inside wall.

"The flowers?" she said, looking hopeful.

Oh, boy, I thought, she's missed the whole package. I pointed to the box once again. "Is there anything in there they could have come from?" Imani still looked blank, but I could see she wanted to find an answer to please me. I pointed to the empty chrysalis. "Do you remember what was in there and just came out?"

"But, Karen, I don't know the word!" she answered patiently and calmly. There it is, I said to myself, she does not know how to name it and therefore cannot even begin to speak about my original question. I gave her the word: *caterpillar*. It was a hard one for her to say, but she tried it several times. I realized that I had used the word *caterpillar* many times with the children, assuming that every child knew the meaning of the word, but I had never had each child say it out loud and slowly. I had forgotten that for Imani, as for many new English speakers, the words I used just blended together and were indistinguishable from one another. I reminded myself to check more carefully for the meaning of the most basic words before I taught anything.

I wondered, though, why, if Imani could not say the word *caterpillar*, she did not just find another way to describe the animal. Perhaps it was a matter of dignity. Imani was very dignified and also very unsure about the scientific way of regarding the world, wanting to please me but not having the language to speak about scientific things.

IMANI IN SECOND GRADE

It is fortunate for me that the children I teach have the opportunity to stay with me for two years. I have yet to see any child who does not benefit from a long term teacher/student relationship and from the deep peer relationships that develop over two years. And certainly as a teacher-researcher, I gain enormous insight when I watch children for two years. Imani returned to my classroom in second grade with a barely concealed eagerness finally to master the difficult process of reading. In first grade she had managed to learn her letters and most of her sounds. She entered second grade still unsure about what the difference was between a letter and a word, but with a much different attitude toward instruction. Within a month she had moved beyond early reading strategies and was rapidly increasing her sight-word vocabulary.

As the second graders became oriented to homework, Imani asked for more, telling me I did not give her enough. When the second graders started a formal spelling program, I hesitated to ask Imani to join us, knowing that she struggled with reading simple words, but she insisted. As the weeks went by, Imani became the queen of spelling with a streak of perfect tests, while the native English-speaking children lagged behind.

She began to take great pleasure in writing, meticulously developing her own style of script, which only she could read. And her interest in science deepened as she participated more actively in our science curriculum, carefully drawing shells in her science journal and writing about the differences between cats and dogs. She was entranced by our discussions and readings from science books about the beginnings of our planet, and she drew a series of pictures in her art and science journals that were careful studies of the illustrations in those books. When I asked her to explain the drawings, she gave me detailed ideas about what they meant. She seemed to be consolidating a very strong visual orientation to all her studies.

By late fall, Imani was a figure of importance and authority in the classroom. It is true that her fierce pride and stubbornness sometimes got in her way; that her love of school rituals had deepened to the point where she was completely intolerant of the shenanigans of the first-grade boys, at times cuffing them on the back of the head when they would not quiet down; and that we still struggled with gaps in her everyday language ("Karen, what is a list?"). But as Thanksgiving approached and Imani prepared to celebrate her first such holiday in this country, her presence helped us to speak about the real meaning of the word *pilgrim*. When I asked the children if any one of them was a pilgrim, they were puzzled, until finally one of them pushed Imani's hand up in the air and the other children seemed in a rush of voices to grasp the meaning of the word, calling out her name. Characteristically, she hid her face in one hand and giggled, but the knowledge was powerful and important for every child.

It is this kind of depth that children like Imani provoke as we more completely absorb their past histories and their adaptations to school. Her story helps me describe the rich spirit that immigrant children often bring to my classroom, a spirit I have become better able to track as I document everyday events and collect the artifacts of their efforts to become part of our class. It also presents some of the more elusive problems that second-language learners, who may have no formal preparation for school subjects, exhibit as they appear to become more proficient in English. It has been my observation as a classroom teacher that just at the point when new English speakers are deemed competent enough to be fully mainstreamed into the classroom, new difficulties with language and curriculum emerge.

Those problems are very subtle and are best illustrated by Imani's emerging misunderstanding of the finer points of language usage; for example, her bewilderment over the kinds of words and phrases that relate to higher-level thinking, words such as *reptiles, mammals, list, grouping, neighborhood*, and *pilgrim*. Just as the immigrant child finds utilitarian and functional language within reach, he or she begins to meet obstacles to achieving real intellectual integration. Although the support Imani received from our English as a second language teacher, which totaled about 45 minutes per day, enabled her to assimilate quickly into the culture of the classroom, in her second year, when she was no longer receiving those services, she and I began to struggle in every area of the curriculum with the more complex parts of language. For all practical purposes, Imani could not effectively participate in group discussions about bigger questions, and her ineffectiveness in contributing to these discussions limited my ability to see whether she was understanding our studies. Only because she had access to extensive drawing materials, and time to use them, did I realize how deep her interest in science and social studies was.

For example, her detailed drawings of the changing earth and of a bird (Figure 3.5) show her to be a keen observer of detail and an avid student of science. The artistic process enabled Imani and me to speak further about ideas that might have intrigued her in a science lesson but that she would have been unable to pursue in a discussion. Moreover, when in a movement session I asked the children to create a pattern with a three-part repetition, Imani, who could not in any clear way explain what a pattern was or why a picture could be said to have a pattern, could create a complex and innovative dance quite superior to any other. As I discovered with Jiana, providing opportunities for creative action gives children who

Figure 3.5. Sketch of a bird in Imani's science journal.

are less facile with dominant language forms a chance to communicate about themselves and their most important concerns.

Imani's story as a learner, which was more clearly revealed because she had access to many forms of communication, gives further evidence that all classrooms must be places where children can leave trails, as it were, trails that help them to fully reveal themselves and that in turn help the teacher follow the path of their learning and their talents. In furthering this process, every member of our classroom community is prodded to think about the resilience and bravery of children like Imani and about their powerful and sometimes voracious desire to communicate and learn. We are constantly reminded through their presence that language must be used with clarity and care and that the act of being schooled, of belonging to a class of children and attending school daily, is a privilege rather than a burden.

4

"Bad" Boys in the Classroom

Have you ever been in a sunny field
when the dragon flies buzzzzzz
and the grass turns green?

Have you seen the lake that runs
into a small quiet stream
with fish

and trees that sparkle in the sun?
And the rabbits jump
and run free?

But it's all in me.

William, age 7

This chapter is a politically incorrect one. Its subject matter swings from the domain of children such as Imani, who begin their educational career from a point of disadvantage, to consider the worldview of the most privileged children in our society. In it, I look at the ways in which some boys, through their use of language, attempt to control the dynamics of the classroom, and in that process silence many other children. I also describe what I, as a student of children's narratives who has struggled to see these boys in a different light, have learned about "bad" boys in the context of my classroom. I plan to plead the "bad" boy's case, arguing that they are an underserved and misunderstood classroom population. That, in itself, is a grossly unpopular stance. Clearly, most studies of what does not happen for girls in the classroom focus on what does happen for boys, at the girls' expense. Those studies imply that teachers inadvertently or intentionally favor boys, and they cite, for example, observations of boys receiving more teacher attention and more positions of responsibility in the classroom. I propose to look at what does *not* happen for these particular boys as one of the main reasons that girls are silenced and underserved.

51

(Although I will not continue to use quotation marks around the word *bad* for the remainder of this chapter, it is important to note that I am using the term *bad* as a stereotype, implying a public image rather than a true portrait of these boys.)

Like much of my work, this piece of research begins in my own life: My son, as an elementary and high school student, often played the role of a bad boy. He was not bad in the pathological sense, because bad boys are not violent boys; they are not boys with serious mental health issues; they do not hurt people physically. In fact, bad boys are somewhat revered in this culture. They are like James Dean, Marlon Brando, and Elvis Presley. They are the little Calvins of "Calvin and Hobbes" (Figure 4.1). As a phenomenon, they make us nervous, because bad boys are very interested in power of all sorts and usually are not nice boys. In schools, they control classrooms in very subtle ways. In families, they alternately cause consternation and self-conscious delight. My son was the first child to teach me about bad boys from the bad boy's perspective.

For a long time I mistook my own child's bad boy role in school as a mixture of very calculated rebelliousness and frustration over the restrictions of classrooms. He rejected most of what schools had to offer him, did not follow school rules, disrupted classes, and resented any limits put on his time that were school-related. By his sophomore year in high school, he was cutting as many classes as possible and doing only the minimum amount of work to attain grades that kept him on the college track. Yet by all accounts this was a very bright, articulate, creative, and deep-thinking child who should have done well in school. He clearly felt school was not designed for him.

As he progressed through high school, and I began to think more and more about bad boys, I noticed that he had ways of processing information that were oppositional to the ways most of his teachers expected him to learn. He read books too carefully for meaning, preferring to uncover deeper themes rather than details of plot and character; he found it hard to read a text to answer specific questions; and he thought about main ideas too widely and in a divergent way, which made it hard for him to take objective tests. He evaluated and synthesized rather than analyzed: The big picture and big ideas were more exciting to him than their component parts. He did not remember details, would not use formulas, and usually would not do homework because he said it trivialized the subject matter. He resented putting things on paper to prove that he knew them, could not make an outline for an essay, and did not seem able to edit papers in a thorough way. Most of his teachers attributed his failings, as I did, to laziness, and most were extremely frustrated by the potential they saw slipping away.

Figure 4.1. Calvin, a bad boy, and his perception of school.

I also remembered, as I thought more carefully about his relationship to school, that from the very early days of his education he resented having to go. He wanted to stay home with me or go to day care. If he went to school, it was for his friends; the rest was generally not of interest. He left me, as a parent, in a state of despair because I saw for many years that he did not fit into what I believe was, and is, a very good school system. The work that he preferred to do was his work. The books that he wanted to read were not on any reading list for any class he was in; they were books of his own choosing. If he was supposed to be writing his senior paper on Faust, he would get up early in the morning, write a paragraph, and then settle on the couch to read Henry Miller. I threw my hands up in desperation over and over again. What was I supposed to think? Which work should have been more important for him — the school's work, or his own? And how did this struggle of opposition begin?

Finally, as I began to think more systematically about the bad boys I taught, I noticed that the boys who tried each year to disrupt my class were very much like my son. I start school each year rested and filled with excitement about my new class. Inevitably, two or three days into the new semester, I begin to tangle with one boy, and sometimes many boys. By the second week I may find myself unable to control a discussion about a story book, or call the class to order, and when I look for the cause of that struggle I find it rests in my interactions with the bad boys in my class.

WHAT ARE BAD BOYS REALLY LIKE?

The struggle for control always takes me by surprise and is always present to differing degrees. It is something that teachers come to expect as part of their job, and it is also the hardest work we do. There is, moreover, a more serious problem that this struggle underscores, and that is that it takes time away from teaching and learning. It impedes the process for all the children in the class; it depletes the teacher's energy, enthusiasm, and time. As I became more worn down by the struggle to understand my son's bad boy behavior, I also lost patience with the struggle in school. Two years ago, I decided to explore the thinking and actions of these children and began, very self-consciously, documenting their stories. Why do I use the word *self-consciously* here? Most probably because I had the uncomfortable feeling that I might be part of the problem.

What are bad boys really like? As I have tracked their behavior and actions in the classroom, and compared those with my son's persona both at school and at home, certain consistencies have emerged. Unlike the picture most teachers (including, initially, myself) have of them as uninterested, egocentric learners, these children are often very creative, deep thinkers who have an absolute love for meaty curricula. Most are sensitive and in some ways feminine in their soft-spokenness, but they also love loud noise, yelling, pushing and shoving, and intense physicality. They often find school hard in that they do not really want to follow *my* ideas of what they ought to learn; and although they are eventually very successful at it and learn to do it, they always resist any efforts to make learning routine or disciplined.

They become voracious readers who do not want to parse up their literature to fill in worksheets and answer comprehension questions. They are often storytellers with a very mischievous and naughty agenda. Many of them dislike required writing assignments and scribble all over their papers, filling them with erasures and crossing out, but they love to do meticulous handwriting exercises, and sometimes, when their muse gets the better of them, they burst out with the most lyrical and poetic writing or language, such as the poem that opens this chapter. They are every student teacher's nightmare, and they will do everything in their power to be the baddest of the bad boys: throw things, turn their back on teachers, start fights, talk out of turn, talk out of turn, talk out of turn. Often talk is one of their prime weapons.

I have found that these boys have many qualities that I, as a teacher, admire and work to cultivate. They are traits that I believe are important for all learners. Yet even if these boys become more engaged in my classroom, they retain those bad boy characteristics that drive other teachers to sterner means of control. Some end up spending almost every music, art, and even gym class in the office sitting on the bench because they are so disruptive, especially when the teachers are women. They find themselves under constant scrutiny and control. The child gains little, often being ejected from a class he likes, and the teacher dreads his appearance in class. All teachers recognize bad boys when they see them, and they know they are trouble.

I now believe that these boys, for many complex reasons, work to control the dynamics of a classroom, determining its discourse style, teacher management strategies, and hidden agendas. I have begun to envision them as little meteorites that are flung from outer space into the microcosm of the classroom. And in some cases, depending on the personality of the teacher and the style of the school, they are never pulled into the classroom orbit, choosing instead to bounce from side to side, wobbling and crashing into the other orbiting bodies, always resisting the pull of gravity into the center of the classroom community. This metaphor plays itself out with these boys disrupting and changing the adaptive patterns of many other children in the classroom, sometimes for years: silencing some children, harassing others, and distracting many. I wonder, now, what makes school so hard for these children and whether they are going to end up like my son—spending years and years unhappily in an institution that is a bad fit. What is it in the relationship between these boys and school that creates their dilemma, a dilemma that I intuitively believe can become a script for the way they will live out their lives. How can I, as a teacher, explore their point of view as learners and pull them into the mainstream of the classroom?

As I have thought about bad boys, I have collected their stories, some of them sharing-time fake stories, some taken from their writing, some stories that they have told in plays or dances, and some I see unfolding on the playground. Many of these stories have no words but imply how these boys position themselves in relation to the world. Many of these stories contradict the common observation of the bad boy as the spoiler, the child who deliberately disrupts classroom activities. All of them portray children whose needs as learners directly contradict the structure of most schools as we know them. In presenting each of them I have combined a description of the child with excerpts from my field notes.

Alex

Alex is a child who is pegged as a bad boy before his mouth even opens. Usually dressed in a black turtleneck and jeans with cowboy boots on his feet, his unsmiling face and closely cropped hair give him the air of someone to be reckoned with. He bristles easily at the slightest affront from another child, often striking out with his elbows and scowling menacingly. As a student, he is at first sullen and often unresponsive, becoming easily frustrated at repetitive tasks or writing assignments. He detests the transitions between subjects that take him away from his intense trains of thought and often refuses to put away one piece of work to begin another.

At recess, I can usually spot Alex out on the edges of the playground, holding a huge branch or stick aloft, leading a line of boys on some mysterious chase across the playground. Later he will be crouched on the ground using the stick to dig a hole in the turf. Leaves, twigs, and branches will pile up as Alex and friends build imaginary structures. Often teachers, including myself, will reprimand Alex for the way in which he carries the sticks and branches. It seems aggressive, almost mirroring Alex's simmering quality, as if the slightest change in intent could make him dangerous.

Yet closer observation reveals a child of great complexity, and sensitivity.

Field Notes: A bassist and a flautist play improvisational jazz in the background as a movement session begins. The children sit quietly, then begin to stir. Alex is up immediately, moving to the quick staccato rhythm. He is in complete control, crossing and criss-crossing the room, weaving in and out of dense groups of children, some of whom are dancing in pairs, his feet moving in quick time to the rapid rhythm. He is like a flamenco dancer, dressed in black as usual, facing first this way then that, body twisting and turning, hands pushing the space away in angular and fluid strokes, eyes unseeing, face still. This is truly a dancer: transfixed and transported. He is body and mind moving through space.

Each morning as the children draw in their art journals, I notice that Alex always works alone, a box of Craypas laid out neatly in front of him. He draws with broad sweeping strokes, creating designs with bold colors and simple forms. Alex spends a great deal of time choosing colors, using the Craypas to blend and shade, juxtaposing shades that would seem to have no relationship but that work in his compositions. When other children come by to speak to him, he ignores them. The process is completely silent and focused.

Saya brings in a basket of Shepherd's Purse wildflowers to share. She shows us how to snap each seed pod back, turn the stem upside down, and shake it to make a rattle. She gives each child a long stem, and they make their own rattles. We are all delighted with this trick, and questions and comments follow. After a few minutes, I look up and notice that Alex has taken his spray of flowers and draped it around his head like a wreath. The flowers dangle below his ears like earrings. He reminds me of Dionysus getting ready to travel the Greek countryside.

Earl, our pet cockatiel, is perched on Alex's shoulder as I read a story. Alex sits very still and listens raptly to the story, as is his habit. Suddenly, Alex starts to moan and cry silently, his hands still in his lap and his shoulders hunched. I stop and ask him what's wrong. He points to the bird, who is pecking at a mole on his neck. Apparently the bird thinks the mole is something to eat. Alex continues to cry but does not push or strike the bird, as he would a child. Another child lifts the bird off his shoulder and hands it to Anita, my intern.

Tony

Tony, a tall, strapping boy with striking good looks, is an object of adulation for both boys and girls. At 7, girls relate to him in a coquettish and teasing way, chasing him and then running away. Early in his first-grade year, he ignored them, but as the year progressed I noticed Tony taking on the same suggestive behavior. Boys follow him around adoringly. Some pick fights with him to prove they are stronger. He does not really like to fight and will avoid all-out confrontations if at all possible. He is a quiet, soft-spoken boy who rarely raises his voice.

Tony, however, is a bad boy inside the school. He refuses to participate in group discussions and harasses student teachers, music teachers, art teachers, gym teachers, and substitutes in a number of increasingly subtle ways. He sits in back of the group, talking softly to his friend, ignoring requests to be quiet, turning his body away from a teacher when he is addressed. Often he will not do work for teachers other than myself, instead choosing to distract other children by stealing their crayons or pencils, grabbing their papers, or throwing food. By second grade, Tony's bad boy behaviors are becoming more refined. Rather than talking over a teacher, he will sit like a statue in the group, drumming his fingers on the floor or table and making soft, only slightly audible clicking sounds. That, alone, is enough to get him ejected from an art or music class.

I have noticed, however, that, like Alex, Tony is an actor, a dancer, and an artist. He spends most of his free time alone or at a table with a few friends, meticulously sketching fantasy figures in his art journals and rarely, if ever, choosing color. During this process Tony is completely introverted, responding only occasionally as his friends chat around him. He is silent and engrossed in the art, and brings each finished drawing to me for discussion and comment. (Figures 4.2 and 4.3)

Field Notes: Monday afternoon, and we are dancing to the music of the Paul Winter Consort. The children have listened to a particular piece of music several times and I have posed the problem of constructing a dance to the music with a partner, using a three-part repeating pattern in which each part builds on a movement from the last. Tony and Donald have teamed up and are over in a corner of the small gym arm in arm. I am not sure who is leading and who isn't, but they begin to dance a tango-like waltz, moving blithely around the room with a combination of taps, high goose steps, and twisting skips. Tony looks like Fred Astaire in a baseball cap: tall, elegant, face frozen in a dignified smile as he and Donald move around the edges of the floor.

Figure 4.2. Tony's sketch from his art journal.

The class is developing an improvisational play based on a story they wrote that is a bizarre spinoff of Little Red Riding Hood and the character of a wolf in sheep's clothing. Tony jumps at the part of the 90-year-old salamander, and as we begin rehearsal he is radiant, entering the scene stooped and leaning on an invisible cane, his voice quavering, but loudly belligerent. I notice as he improvises his lines, giving advice to the sheep who has been accused of being a wolf in sheep's clothing, that he sounds like he is missing his teeth. Indeed, as he stoops over Sam, wagging his finger in his face, I see that his cheeks are sucked in in a toothless grin, and his eyes are squinting myopically. Tony *is* the old salamander!

On the playground Tony is sought after for his size and physical abilities. For three warm fall days, I sit at recess watching the boys at play. Tony is in the middle of 20 or so boys, aged 6, 7 and 8. They

Figure 4.3. Another sketch from Tony's art journal.

are playing what, for lack of a better term, I call their Kicking-Tripping-Pull the Punch and Falling Game. Tony has his wind-breaker in his hand and is using it as a fairly harmless whip. Two boys approach him from both sides, trying to trip him from the back and side. As they come closer, Tony stands perfectly still, legs far apart, hand with the jacket outstretched, face immobile, baseball cap shielding his eyes. (I'm sure they can't see where he's looking.) The boys hesitate, but move in, and as one tries to trip him, the other grabs his shoulders and begins to wrestle. Tony moves very little, pre-vailing through his serious advantage in size. He wrestles one boy to the ground and begins to chase the other with his jacket. The first boy tackles him from behind, and they hit the ground hard and roll. Tony and the boy jump up, brush themselves off, turn their backs on one another and head for another part of the field. Not one word has been spoken.

Michael

Michael brought a reputation from kindergarten as a spoiler: a child who was mean-spirited, used foul language, and disrupted other children's activities. In the first few weeks of school, his reputation was confirmed. I found myself once again struggling to establish who was in charge of the classroom. Michael used language with great skill; he understood that anyone's words could be trivialized by maintaining a running commentary in the background. His voice was always audible during the reading of a story or the process of discussion, whether led by an adult or a child. He rarely had anything positive to say about a child's or a teacher's ideas. I found myself having to be very explicit with him about when he could or could not talk. He spent a great deal of time sitting in a chair, banned from group meetings.

Michael's presence in our class would not have been so disruptive if he had received no response from the other children. However, his one-person conversations usually prompted other children to reply, either to his remarks about another child's inadequacy, or to his plays on words (which were quite impressive in their complexity), or to his off-color and suggestive jokes. I found his intrusions into the talk space of other children especially disturbing, as one might expect from a teacher who so carefully creates room for extended discussion, and so I resisted his efforts for a few weeks. Finally, however, I decided not to be the policewoman of sharing time and stopped guarding other children's right to be heard. I wondered what would happen if I was not the authority figure. (One might wonder why, after two years of documenting sharing-time formats in which the teacher is silent, I had to reexplore this issue. Still, in those two years, the behavioral composition of the class had been quite different in that the children seemed to understand and follow my lead as a respectful observer. The new first graders, however, did not have the same response. They had learned in kindergarten to follow Michael's lead, and they were playing that out once again.)

Quite quickly, when the children realized that neither Anita, my intern, nor I would monitor their behavior, the second graders made their reactions to Michael's talk explicit. They shushed him and complained, would not call on him for questions and comments, and, when it was his day to tell a story, did not respond to his story in the ways he had seen when I was taking a more active role. He was somewhat mollified by their subdued response, and his attempts to dominate classroom discussions diminished. He seemed to be trying to figure out how to act.

Concurrently, I began to look carefully at Michael's work in art journals and writing. I noted that he was a remarkable artist with very fine motor control and a mature sense of perspective. Again, as did Alex and Tony, he spent much of his free time alone, drawing in his art journal. He, too, was fascinated with fantasy and mythological figures and would engage me in elaborate discussions of the background and story of his pictures (Figure 4.4). His writing was quite fluent and descriptive, ranging wide in the topics he covered and the style of presentation. Further, when he was involved in these activities he was absolutely absorbed in the process, usually working well beyond the allotted time. He also showed an extensive grasp of scientific information, which he would happily relate to different questions under discussion, usually at inappropriate times. Often Michael's energy and knowledge, which were obviously unusual for a child his age, went unsupported by myself or other children, because he had no apparent sense of how and when to present them, choosing to intrude on discussions rather than make a more subtle entry.

I noticed these things but could not see any coherence in them until I began science talks in early October.

> *Field Notes:* As we begin our weekly science talks, I am somewhat apprehensive about how the open-ended structure of the talks will work with Michael as a participant. He still has great trouble censoring the words that come out of his mouth, even though both Anita and I have been sitting with him in group discussions, coaching him as to what is and is not acceptable to say in public. The question under consideration for our first science talk is: How did animals begin? The children sit in a circle, and I am silent, taking notes as usual. As the discussion begins, the children are extremely settled. Early on in the talk Michael, who is sitting next to Anita, gets up on his knees and Anita and I make eye contact. I know we are both wondering what that movement signals. As I watch, it becomes clear that his erect posture mirrors an intellectual excitement that he can barely contain.
>
> Michael speaks frequently in the talk, maintaining an earnest and wide-eyed attitude. He shows an unusual interest in adopting parts of other children's thoughts, and expanding them, and is effusive in his praise for others, at one point saying with great excitement, "I think Camille and Ian are both right! And well, I think Camille's very, I think Camille's pretty right!" This is a little shocking because usually nothing he says about most of the other children in the class is positive.

Figure 4.4. Michael's drawing of a mythological character.

On the Thursday before Halloween, Michael and three other first graders express an interest in making pumpkin muffins with me and a graduate student who is observing in our class. When his name is called, he leaps up and races across the classroom, roughly pushing the other children aside in a rush to be first to reach the cooking area. Just as I move to reprimand him and pull him aside to let the other children walk ahead, I notice the look on his face and the urgency in his posture. It is the look of the science talk. His eyes are wide open, his mouth breathless — he can barely contain his excitement and delight. I catch the words I would have said, chastising him for pushing and running, and realize that I am just beginning really to see Michael: a fiercely intelligent and eager child who is unable to moderate his response to new challenges and new subject matter.

Michael has plugged himself into the listening station and is listening to a tape of our last science talk with three other children. Every time he hears a new voice, his own booms out over all sounds in the classroom: "Tony, it's you!" — and he reaches for Tony, who is playing a math game at a nearby table. Tony, silent as usual, looks over at him, looks at his card partner, and rolls his eyes at me.

"Oh, no, it's Charles!" — and he points to Charles, who is nearby playing a game of Othello with Soo Kim, and pulls at his shirt. Charles scowls and shrugs his shoulder.

"Wow, listen! This time it's Ariel!" She is also listening to the tape and smiles. As usual, Michael's voice has begun to disrupt any sense of order that we had achieved. I give him the sign to bring his voice down, and once again I see his face: He is tremendously excited and absolutely awash with delight.

Charles

Charles, barely 6 in September, entered first grade as one of the youngest children in our class. He dressed each day like an athlete, with sweatshirt and matching pants and a baseball cap that never left his head. To see his eyes, I would push the cap slightly up so that we could speak. The early weeks in first grade were tough for Charles, and he made sure I knew it. The day was long. He had to sit and listen to other people talk. Kids kept saying how little he was, and to top it off, I did not seem to find his jokes to be very funny. For my part, what I saw was a very cute little boy who often was not very nice.

After two years of thinking about and watching bad boys operate, I realized that Charles fit the model very well. I knew what was going on for him. He had trouble ceding control of the class to me and Anita. When we were in the chair attempting to teach, lead a discussion, or read a book, Charles and his friend Michael would provide a constant stream of interjections about what was being said or read. The chatter was constant, and it was not appreciative. It ranged from comments on how bored they were, to how they already knew what we were saying, to off-color jokes about bathroom functions or sex. The comments were intended to grab the attention of the other children, and they did. Inevitably, the other first graders responded to what they were saying and began conversations of their own, causing us to stop what we were doing and try to regain control. How, in fact, could anyone not respond to Charles's comment following a reading of the Hans Christian Anderson story of the Little Mermaid.

"Oh, rats," he said as he leaned back into Anita's lap, "I thought the ending would have sex in it."

"What do you mean, sex?" responded Tom.

"*You* know," answered Charles.

"He means, like kissing and stuff, right, Charles?" offered another first grader.

"Nooooo," answered Charles.

"Noooo," continued Michael, "he means like bras and stuff, right, Charles?"

That was a typical exchange, and I had come to understand from my observations of bad boys that what Charles was doing was very predictable. In his attempts to control the dynamics of the group, his main strategy was to control the talk of the group. However, being only 6, he was somewhat obvious in his strategy, not having had the practice and experience of Tony. Charles also used his talk and his nonverbal communications to take the attention from other children as well as from me and Anita. If another child was volunteering an idea or sitting in the chair telling a story, Charles would continue his comments and jokes. Sometimes he would use obvious gestures, such as two thumbs down or holding his nose, to indicate what he thought of that person's ideas. What was most disturbing to me, though, was his choice of targets for his comments. They were usually girls.

In fact, Charles was so unpracticed in the subtleties of being a bad boy that he constantly presented me with an opportunity to track the thinking and attitude, if not the origin, of the bad boy mentality. He was amazingly willing to talk about what he was thinking. After one particularly difficult day when he had been using a lot of bathroom talk and making fun of other children, I sat down to confirm with Charles that I would have to call his parents and speak with them about his behavior in school. I explained that it was very important to use words respectfully in my classroom. Charles did not capitulate. He rolled his eyes, pulled his baseball cap farther down, and continued to make jokes. Finally, he said,

"Well, I don't even have to go to school, you know."

"I hate to say it, Charles, but it's the law," I answered. "You have to go to school."

"No way," he threw back over his shoulder, and he turned his chair away from me. "Then," he continued, "I'll go to Pierce School."

"Do you think you can talk this way at Pierce?" I asked.

"Probably not," said Charles. "But it's a better school. I been there once for LEDP (the after-school program), and I liked it."

From my point of view, this conversation signaled something of a turning point. Charles seemed to understand that what I was really objecting to in his behavior was his use of language, and he also came to the sad and public realization that he had to go to school. School was compulsory, and although he objected to that, it did put my role in perspective. I was all he had to work with, and I was trying to strike a deal with him.

As the days passed through October, Charles gained more control over his language when he was involved in whole-class activities, but, as I was to discover, he would find new ways to express his attitude towards me and other children in the class.

Field Notes and Transcript: One morning in October on his designated sharing day, Charles gets into the chair and indicates that he will be telling a fake story.

CHARLES: We went to Alaska . . . And Michael, both Michaels, they were walking behind me, and suddenly, Michael T. fell on top of me, and fell in the iceberg . . . And then, Alex, he, we saw a cow, and Alex, and I saw a cow, and Alex went like muscle man, and picked it up, and by accident . . . he fell . . . and *he* fell in its mouth, and then when the, when the cow had to go bathroom, Alex came out as *manure* . . . And then Katy, I mean Dora, I mean Imani (*laughs*) she fell on top of him, and knocked him and Imani fell to Mars. She got a lot more . . . and she fell to Jupiter and then she felt stupiter. And then, Ka-, I mean Camille, she . . . she fell, she . . . Alex punched her all the way to Mars. And then Michael, he took and the whole class, *they* jumped on Alex so they could go all the way. Alex punched them all the way to Texas.

MICHAEL: Me, me all the way to Texas.

ALEX: Darn, I wanted Mars.

CHARLES: And then Michael, he was, when he showed up there he was going, "Yee hawwww!" on the horsie, and then Tom —

TOM: Oh, oh.

CHARLES: Oh, oh is right.

(As Charles continues his commentary, his voice is getting much louder, as if he is gaining momentum.)

CHARLES: Tom was at a bull rodeo, was at a rodeo, and Tom had to say his prayers before he got killed. Tom, before the thing killed him, he went to sewercide. I mean, *he* got killed, and Tom went to sewercide.

TOM: What are you talking about?

(Tom, a second grader who is sitting close to the front of the group, is clearly unhappy with the direction the narrative has taken. He is scowling and muttering to himself. As I listen on the outskirts of the group, I am also becoming slightly uncomfortable with the content of the narrative. Although Charles has left behind his carefully cloaked bathroom humor, which began the story, it seems as if his narrative is becoming more and more violent.)

CHARLES: Committed sewercide, and then, Tom, I mean Dora, she had to say her prayers before she came out in horse manure. She came out as manure, and then she was stepped on. And then, everyone followed Tony to the scientist's place and then they got shrunk. And then, Alex was too small, and Eli was too small to go, so he stayed home and got chicken pox, by a chicken. And he was a chicken egg. And he went "Pock, pock! Pock, pock!" And then Michael T., he took Alex' butt, and went — ready set, Alex — and kicked him all the way to Mars . . . where he got more bras.

MICHAEL: Charles, can I kick somebody all the way to Mars? Like Karen?

CHARLES: O.K. And Anita was kicked all the way to Jupiter, and she felt a little stupiter.

ALEX: With Imani.

CHARLES: Yeah with Imani (*laughs*). And especially Ian . . . And then . . . And Hiroyasu, he thought Karen looked like a horse so he jumped on her, and kicked her, whipped her, and whipped her, and whipped her, until she was dead. Then she was as flat as a pancake. Then he took her to a bull.

ANALYSIS

By the second month of school, Charles had obviously figured out that he could maintain his viewpoint and express it publicly if it was couched within an established classroom format, in this case the sharing time that occurred each morning. He was quickly learning the subtleties of classroom discourse and culture, understanding that if the teacher has a standard of acceptable behavior that dampens one form of expressing bad boy anger, there were still ways to push the boundaries of the rules.

During the telling of his fake story, when Charles had begun to kill me off, the other children became visibly restless, glancing nervously over at me, realizing, I think, that he was pushing the boundaries too far. I, however, was trying to maintain a completely impassive posture, taking notes as usual and watching Charles carefully. I have to admit that my internal response was very uneven. On the one hand, Charles was telling a story that I believed was the clearest, most genuine bad boy narrative I had ever heard, and I was secretly elated. On the other hand, as the story escalated in aggressiveness and I became the ultimate target, I was appalled at the extent of his anger and the directness of the violence. It is only too easy to extrapolate from the fantasy of a small six-year-old boy the actions of grown men who, when angered, act on those fantasies, with women and children as their victims.

This, of course, is the crux of the problem of bad boys. For myself as a female teacher, what they present are expressions of the undercurrents of sexual politics in our society. I believe these young boys have acquired, by a very early age, deep and what seems at times to be unconscious needs to play out over years of schooling a struggle for dominance over other children and the powerful women they encounter. At the same time I also have experienced the immediate and very strong reactions of their female teachers, who, to a person, describe how laden with meaning and how disruptive the smallest gesture, well-placed groan, or word of these boys can be. Tony's drumming of his fingers on the floor while his teacher tries to present a lesson, if taken out of context, means nothing. Charles's interest in bathroom language might be attributed to immaturity. Teachers intuitively know that the struggle is about power, and, eventually, so do the boys. How else am I to interpret my own son's delight in the response he could get from substitute teachers by wearing his baseball cap slung low over his eyes, or, as he enthusiastically related to me one day, the struggle that was precipitated in an English class when he casually placed his hand on a friend's knee (a female friend, but still only a friend) and tipped his chair back ever so slightly?

What is most disturbing about this dilemma, though, is that the bad boys I see exhibit many androgynous traits. They are, in a Jungian sense, very aware of the anima, the feminine, in their lives. As youngsters they place it quite visibly in front of their teachers if they are offered the opportunity. They dance, paint, sing, draw, write poems, speak in make-believe languages, and adorn themselves with flowers. They take pleasure in many activities normally associated with girls' pastimes; for example, taking great care to fashion elaborate Valentine boxes covered with hearts, lace, flowers, and pictures of monsters. They become fiercely devoted to their teachers, sometimes deliberately spurning any new adults in a classroom.

Yet research studies repeatedly assert, and teachers are told, that the unequal status of women and girls in the classroom is the result of intentional or ignorant practices by teachers (most of whom are female) that limit or impede equal educational opportunity for females. Most often cited are the disproportionate amounts of teacher support and attention that boys receive in classrooms as compared with girls, or the physical proximity teachers maintain with boys, or the greater access to leadership roles that boys attain. These kinds of generalizations seem simplistic to me. Certainly it may be true that boys receive more attention than girls and that teachers struggle to place them in leadership roles. But I am extremely uncomfortable with the simplistic interpretations of teacher behaviors and the blanket condemnation that those interpretations make of the many teachers, like myself, who consciously work for equity in our classrooms.

What is more true in my own experience as a teacher is that the classroom is only a mirror reflecting the problems of discrimination, misunderstanding, and violence that our society harbors. I question whether these bad boys are acting out their own agendas or simply the tumultuous and divisive agendas they have gleaned from their observations of the world around them. I wonder which boys classroom researchers have been observing so closely in their monitoring of teacher response and their search for equitable practices. Is it every boy, or only a select and dominant few? From my observations, the "good" boys receive as little attention as most of the "good" girls. I also wonder whether the research findings might not simply be exposing the kinds of classroom dynamics that are set in motion by bad boys and their teachers, dynamics that do impede the educational process for the other children but that are the result of complex interpersonal and societal relationships rather than bad teaching.

By looking carefully at the stories of bad boys, I have been able to change my response to their actions. My response has moved from a purely visceral, defensive reaction toward a child who threatens my ability to control a class, to one of examining what that child is telling me about his needs as a learner and his view of the world. What I find is that bad boys require, and thrive in, a classroom that offers expanded opportunities for creative action in all its forms and deep involvement with the content of the curriculum — *and that is true of all children.* When I work to find ways to pull these boys into the center of the classroom community by encouraging them to be comfortable with themselves as learners for whom creative expression is a way of being, *all children are encouraged to find comfort in that way of being.*

By paying close attention to the stories they tell, draw, dance, write, and enact, I am more able to include their divergent worldview in the culture of the classroom. My hope, as they see that school is not a battle-ground, is that they will begin to alter their picture of where their own personal power lies. In the end, I want these boys to experience how powerful it is to belong and fully commit oneself to the creation of a dynamic learning community, where, rather than struggling continuously to assert their superiority and control, they work to fuel the intensity and excitement of everyone's participation.

PART II

Stories about Science

As a child I never talked about science with anyone. In fact, I have little or no recollection of even studying science until I was in high school, and then I did it badly and with great anxiety. I do recall, though, spending a great deal of time outdoors, wandering around the fields and beaches alone, looking, listening, and thinking about things, not science particularly, just about "things." These were completely solitary activities. No one I knew ever talked about science.

It was not until I began to consider what it meant to teach science within an environment where understanding the child's point of view was the teacher's most important task that I started to consider what, exactly, science was. My answer at that time was to provide a science-rich environment, that is, to furnish my classroom with the stuff of the natural world: animals, plants, rocks, water, dirt, and so on. Somehow I knew from my own childhood wanderings that those things held a powerful attraction for children. I also knew that teachers were supposed to ask timely and insightful questions that provoked thinking and hypothesizing in children, and so I did that, too. I think I was moderately successful.

After many years, I also realized that the most exciting things that occurred in my classroom were those things that I did not plan but that I allowed to happen. Some of those things occurred in group meetings where my goal was simply to talk with the children. Some took place spontaneously through the children's interactions with materials, and some occurred through the more introverted processes of writing or making art. In most of these cases, my influence was limited. It might best be described as coaching. These were the moments when the children expressed an insight that, from my vantage point, went beyond the boundaries of their age or circumstances. How did I respond? I stopped placing limits on my ideas of what children could or could not understand, and I began to believe that all children were able to respond to difficult ideas and a wide variety of subjects.

When I was in my early 30s, several important events occurred in my life. After finishing work on a degree, I spent several months in the west of Ireland in a very remote area doing "nothing." I came back from that place feeling as if I had rediscovered a part of my childhood. I was deeply moved by the natural environment and by the hours I spent alone wandering through it and wondering about it. The doing "nothing" of my childhood was reclaimed for its original purpose: that of being awestruck by the diversity and beauty of the natural world. It was also at about this time that I seriously took up writing as a way to think about things, and I found that much of my writing was about the natural world. Gradually, as I put more time into the writing, it turned to poetry and metaphorical stories, and I found I was better able to capsulize my perceptions and my thinking through the medium of metaphor. My silent wanderings were being reclaimed in the written word.

Natural science became my fascination and it began to permeate my teaching, but what was new in this was that I had become more aware of the presence of my own inner dialogue about the world, and I was also able to talk and wonder aloud with young children — and we were speaking the same language! That language was not confined to "scientific" talk; it was poetic, visual, analogic, kinetic. Both personally and professionally, the discovery was liberating. So it seems natural that some of my early work as a teacher-researcher focused on the language of science. I wanted systematically to explore how children talked and wrote about science before they were influenced by the teaching of science, and so I introduced the structure of science journals and science talks into the regular routines of my classroom.

As my research on how children think and talk about science continues, I have become much more able to think about the complexities of the language the children are using. I now see, from my own forays into metaphoric thinking about the natural world, that children's thinking reflects a natural ability to express scientific understandings through imagery and analogy and that it is very difficult for most adults to follow that thinking. I also see that though every child thinks deeply about the world, not all children naturally identify their serious musings with the world of science. Somehow for them science is something mysterious and vague, and their life has nothing to do with the subject. But until a teacher perceives that point of view and works with it, those children remain relatively unable to benefit from science instruction, much as I did as a student. If you cannot place science smack in the middle of the context of your life, how can you ever see yourself as a scientist? If you cannot associate the wonder that the natural world evokes with the excitement of science, how can you dare to ask the silent questions that follow the wondering? Without teachers who bring your questions and wonder and awe into the science classroom, you remain a passive and uncommitted student, someone who is constantly deferring to the authority of other, more scientific individuals.

Yet children's stories about science are, I believe, the most easily obtained. Their questions and theories, when solicited, almost ooze out of them. They are hungry for meaty discussions in which their ideas, rather than the teacher's, are given precedence. Once stated, those ideas offer teachers rich material for teaching. Complex theories, rich metaphors, amazing misconceptions, and passionate questions are offered up, and when those ideas are acted on by the teacher, children begin to see that the study of science is about their lives: Science becomes one more way to expand their evolving story about their world.

This second part of the book explores children's stories about science as I have obtained them through our use of science journals and science talks. Chapter 5 introduces the use of the journals and talks in a general way, providing a theoretical foundation for my use of the talks and describing how they evolved in my classroom. Chapter 6 focuses on one child's struggle to understand the world of science and the ways in which the science journal helped him to talk and write himself into that world. Chapter 7 goes more deeply into children's use of metaphoric language in the science talks and provides an analysis of how metaphor and analogy are used to develop sophisticated theories. Each chapter continues to explore how children use stories to contextualize their experiences in the classroom, and each chronicles how the process of making sense of those stories has changed my understanding of teaching and learning.

5

Making Thinking Visible

Trees have leaves. In the fall, the leaves fall off the trees. And chlorophyll goes up to the top of the whole entire tree. But when it gets colder, the chlorophyll has difficulty getting to the top of that tree, so the chlorophyll stays down for the winter, and on the next page you will find and learn more about trees.

Vera, age 6

How do children incorporate their personal understanding of the world into the knowledge they receive in schools? This chapter describes how what began as an effort to assist children in talking and writing about science expanded to become a way of thinking about difficult questions and ideas. My focus on expanding our use of language for thinking is based on the incorporation of children's personal narratives into the study of science. It enables us to celebrate the interrelationships among the different areas of the school curriculum, and it acknowledges the holistic ways in which young children confront the process of education.

When I first implemented what we now call science talks and science journals in my first-grade classroom three years ago, I intended to assist young children in developing both their conceptualization of what science is and their personal identity as young scientists. At the time, my theoretical rationale was based on expanding what I perceived to be the limited domain of classroom science. Generally, the teaching of elementary science is modeled to fit within the established procedures of laboratory science, and schools create structures within classrooms that mimic the laboratory. Many teachers teach children to infer, hypothesize, identify variables, set up experimental models, carry out experiments, describe, record, and explain. In addition, we add another layer of structure by working intensely with textbooks, science kits, and hands-on activities that are intended both to guide the teacher and to assist the child in making the world of science logical and manageable from an informational point of view. In effect, what teachers develop is a structure that makes a seemingly overwhelming field teachable but at the same time defines or bounds the child's approach to and conceptualization of science.

When studying electricity, for example, students might read an excerpt from a textbook, answer questions about the text, and then conduct experiments with batteries and bulbs. In effect, the children learn to complete a circuit and light the bulb, but often they do not make the connections between the experiments and the production of electricity, because the most difficult and basic questions about how electricity is made, and how it is made visible in their world, are rarely articulated.

A THEORETICAL PERSPECTIVE

When describing the practice of science teaching talk in the classroom, Lemke (1990) both decries the limited scope of science talk in the classroom and describes what it might be.

> Just as with learning a foreign language, fluency in science requires practice at speaking, not just listening. It is when we have to put words together and make sense, when we have to formulate questions, argue, reason, and generalize, that we learn the thematics of science. (p. 24)

His analysis includes a call for children to be able to use scientific language for themselves and for teachers to recognize that a scientific theory "is a way of talking about a subject using a particular thematic pattern," rather than a "description of the way the world really is" (p. 126). Lemke's focused work on science talk reinforces the findings of other researchers about the potential of expanded formats for talk in the classroom (Barnes, 1976; Britton, 1990; Bruner, 1986; Cazden, 1988; Hymes and Cazden, 1980; Michaels, 1990).

Barnes (1976) describes the ways in which collaborative talk among peers enabled secondary school students to work through difficult ideas more thoroughly than instances when the teacher was focusing the discussion. He cites the processes of exploratory talk and co-construction of meaning as important components of collaborative discussions and notes that although the talk is messy, it is a time when children are engaged in higher-level thinking. Britton (1990) proposes that informal language among peers aids them in working through new ideas and suggest that expressive talk is more accessible to students, and hence must precede technical talk about science:

It is the language of their own intimate musings, their inner reflections upon experience, that will serve both to bring their common-sense concepts to the point of engagement with the scientific concept, and to carry out the reconciliatory interpretation. (p. 108)

Hymes and Cazden (1980) refer to the importance of narrative thinking as a "form of knowledge," and, as the following comment shows, children regularly weave a story, filled with their "intimate musings," to help themselves think about difficult questions.

Underground is damp. Some insects live underground. I don't know the names of all of them. Do you? I like earthworms. Do you? I like the smells of the ground. Do you? The ground smells damp. In summer the ground is dry, when the soil does not smell. But I still like it. Do you?

(Ronit, age 6)

Although current science teaching structures can be effective in transmitting limited bodies of knowledge about science to children, they overlook one of the key aspects of "doing" science: the relationship between scientific thinking and larger conceptualizations of the world, and indeed the universe, as an object of wonder and questioning. Often, in the early stages of studying a science unit, the students' most important and compelling questions and theories are never voiced, and hence the key concept that underlies the study itself remains obscure. For example, children's observations about lightning, blackouts, and static electricity, as well as their risky experimentation with electrical outlets and appliances may not be called into play in the study of electricity. The many and varied observations they have made about the subject, all of which provide a rich resource for teachers, are untapped.

As a teacher of young children, I have learned that the questions children ask often reflect a very deep effort to understand their world and that their ability to form theories about difficult questions far surpasses my expectations. Through the medium of science talks and science journals, I have seen children develop ways to make their thinking visible in narrative. In doing so, they were more able to clarify what they knew and created an expanded readiness for new information and new insights. Students also gained a stronger identity as scientific thinkers. Writing and talking about difficult ideas, building theories, asking questions — their stance as students of science changed to value their own role as thinkers and knowers.

As my research on the language of science progressed, however, I noticed that the children I taught did not naturally confine their conceptualization of science to include only natural or physical science and they did not communicate in ways that I associated with scientific language. Instead, they began to include narratives in their journals and their science talks that reflected broadly on the world as a whole, on the entire spectrum of life as we know it. Plants, animals, people, culture—virtually every subject became their starting point for thinking, and in the process of presenting that thinking they used oral and written language devices that were sometimes more literary and poetic than expository. Metaphor, analogy, literary allusions to stories and folklore—6- and 7-year-old children were presenting me with ways of thinking and talking about their world that forced me to revise my conceptualization of the purpose and potential of the science journals and science talks. In fact, as I considered the expansiveness of their views of "science," I realized that my thinking about the place of wonder in children's thinking had somehow assumed that children confined their amazement about their world to things scientific. Clearly they were giving me a different message: Everything in their world prompted a deep and reflective response.

Science journals and science talks, by eliciting children's personal narratives, enable them to discover the interrelationships between their world of experience and the many disciplines they study in school. Although it is true that these activities continue to be labeled "science activities," the children and I understand clearly that their purpose is to explore and clarify their thinking in ways that are inclusive of different ways of knowing, ways that include wonder, imagination, and awe.

The cultivation of wonder and its validation in the child, because we know that children come by it naturally, is not generally one of the stated goals of our curricula, but it is one that I believe holds great potential for teachers. Cobb (1977) describes wonder as "a perogative of childhood" that later becomes an "essential instrument in the work of the poet, the artist, or the creative thinker" (p. 27). By recognizing the importance of wonder and imagination in building the child's understanding of the world, we can tap into what Corbin (1969) describes as an "intermediate universe between, on the one hand, the universe of sensory data and the concepts that express their empirically verifiable laws, and, on the other hand, a spiritual universe" (p. 181). Corbin proposes that the universe of the imagination is a place where deep knowledge is obtained through creative action. For children, who have not abandoned the universe of the imagination, who are still filled with wonder and awe, finding ways to study the world that incorporate transcendent modes of thinking becomes an imperative.

By incorporating journals and talks into my curriculum, I hoped to tap into the child's internal conversations, or personal narratives, which I remembered from my childhood as accompanying my exploration of the world and which I often observed in my own children as they wandered alone outside. These conversations with oneself are filled with pondering and surprise; they contain strands of thinking and reasoning rich in association, personification, metaphor, and analogy. They also include what I call invisible questions, that is, unvoiced questions that children form when they encounter a phenomenon that at the time seems inexplicable: a mirage on a hot road, the rainbow of an oil spill on a city street, an encounter with a person from another culture.

Normally in classrooms these narratives are not placed in the public domain. They are rarely voiced within the context of the school day, and hence their potential as powerful tangents of thought is never tapped. Occasionally they find their way into the classroom record through informal discussions, or more subtly, as images in a painting or drawing. [If the child's thinking behind the image is solicited, however, it is clear that the tangent is part of a continuous process of developing related stories that make the world sensible and orderly (Gallas, 1982).] The use of journals and talks, then, was established so that children would identify this type of thinking as an important resource in school. In essence, by developing a formal structure that elicited their personal narratives as an integral part of the curriculum, I hoped to prod the children to make their silent conversations public.

In discussing narrative as a literary genre, Ricoeur (1984) notes that like metaphor, narrative uses "semantic innovation" to take seemingly different and opposed experiences and synthesize them through the development of plot. He characterizes this work as the result of "the productive imagination," and he notes that this process "integrates into one whole and complete story multiple and scattered events" (p. x). Ricoeur's conceptualization reinforces my sense as a teacher that both narrative and the metaphor that is often embedded in narrative enable children to speak about and synthesize diverse aspects of their experience, thus making thinking visible. If left unvoiced, this type of thinking is never crystallized, never shared, and therefore never offered for public view and comment.

SCIENCE JOURNALS

Every September, I introduce the idea of the science journal to my class of 20 or so first graders. Although most of them cannot read, journal keeping has usually been a part of their kindergarten experience, so they understand at once that the journal is their book: a place where their most important thoughts and questions can be recorded. When I talk about keeping a science journal, there is usually a heavy silence. "What is science?" one of the children inevitably asks, and others look at him or her as if everyone knows the answer. Usually I do not respond to that question, because I view the journal as one place where the child can begin to formulate a personal conceptualization of science. Instead I tell the children that the journal is a place to write about things we are thinking about: questions we have about our world, things we wonder about. I ask them to name a few things they have been thinking about, and we begin a list titled: Ideas for our Science Journals. The children usually volunteer topics in science at first. The list includes plants, animals, space, magnets. Then, inevitably, one child asks if people can go on the list, and I add it. Soon children are volunteering new ideas: castles, pyramids, astronauts, houses.

In the beginning of the school year, many children are very tentative in approaching the journal. They are not sure what can go in one. It is as if I am the ultimate authority on what is important enough to think about. But as they begin to work, I point out to them that they must decide. What can go on in the journal, and who decides? Some children, who believe that they are very scientific people, do not hesitate to begin writing about things they know. For them the journal starts as a place to display knowledge: They write about dinosaurs, space, rocks, mammals, and they believe that filling the pages with information is their mission. Other children are less sure. Some, in fact, can barely muster a short entry in their weekly journal time. They may reluctantly draw a picture of a landscape, an animal, or a house, but they are clearly lost. Yet no matter where each child begins, the focus on the journal and the discussions with their peers and me, which eventually amplify every child's use of the journal, lead them to a larger understanding of what science is and how their personal stories can be an important part of their learning process.

For many children, the process of writing in the journal gives them a place to ask questions and then possibly try to answer them. Here are some of the questions they have asked in September and October:

How do scientists know all that they know? Maybe they got teached. Maybe they searched. Maybe they watched. Maybe they thought about it.

Why do birds have feathers? Could birds fly without feathers? There are so much questions and answers that I can't keep track.

How everything is made? It is very hard. It was very hard to make something. Like a watermelon. Something made that and something made that and on and on forever. Maybe when early humans found the things that the old people made, they figured they could make other things.

How did the animals that were living with dinosaurs not die when the dinosaurs died?

The questions continue all year, and soon other ways of signifying stories about their world enter the journals. The children write and then illustrate their ideas. They make sketches and diagrams of something they have read or seen. They write poems about an idea, for example:

Nature

If winter stayed forever
trees and flowers would feel bad
because nature made them promise
that each and every year
after winter the trees would have pretty buds
and then they would turn into pretty leaves
and the flowers would have pretty buds
that would beckon.

(Amy, age 6)

In the journal all children, like this one, use the picture, the poem, or the observation to develop a story about something that seems relevant to their study of their world of experience. For this child, the poem is a way to record her observations of the coming of spring, as well as a vehicle to express her aesthetic sense of the changing of seasons and the wonder of the cycle. Her understanding of the world, which is both metaphoric and realistic, finds a place in the journal, and she expands her conceptualization of how one writes and thinks about science.

Many children move on throughout the year to use the journal as a place to think consecutively about one subject. Often the entries on a subject will continue for several weeks, as shown by the following example, which took three weeks to complete:

How come we are different?
Maybe because of our noses.
Maybe because of our babies.

Maybe because of our faces.
Maybe because of our writing.
Maybe because of our eyes.
Maybe because of our feet.
Maybe because of our lips.
Maybe because of our ears.
Maybe because of our knees.
Maybe because of our tans.
Maybe because of our tastebuds.
Maybe because of our names.
Maybe because of our moles.
Maybe because of our food.
Maybe because of our pupils.
Maybe because of our elbows.
Maybe because of our brains.
Maybe because of our smells.

(Sandy, age 6)

Obviously this child had been thinking long and hard about physical and cultural differences, and she had been carefully watching the people around her. Note also the form the entry takes. It is both a list and a creative composition of the child's reflections on the subject of human differences. Each line is an abbreviated representation of what was clearly a long internal narrative or thinking segment about one human difference. Some children, such as this one, will begin with a fascination early in the year and will return to it periodically as they think and study more. This particular child spent much of the year writing, drawing, and thinking about people: their physiognomy, anatomy, culture, history, and foibles. Another child wrote for weeks in late winter on the subject of dirt, filling pages with a discussion of dirt, weaving into the text its relationship to animals, plants, geography, history, and himself. The following is an example of how his narrative unfolded.

Dirt is one of the most exciting things in all of the country. In the world, there is tons of dirt. Dirt is good for flowers. Worms like it. All kinds of plants and animals like it. Pigs like it. Dirt is even good for pumpkins. Dirt is all over the sea and oceans and seashore. Clams lie around in it. Oysters like it. There is tons of it everywhere. . . . Snakes like it too. They crawl on it. They just love it. Pigs lie around in it all the time like as if they were dead. There was even dirt when the dinosaurs were alive. . . . Once a year seal cows come to the seashore and the males fight, and whoever wins gets to mate with the females. Once they mate they fall in love and soon will get married. They like it, even maybe they even love it. . . . Beaches have lots of it. At the beach you can bury things in it. That's just what pirates did with their gold. . . . Dirt is found all over the world. There is even dirt in Alaska. I love that part of the world. It has sand under the ice. . . .

(Andy, age 7)

For this child the subject of dirt allows his mind to wander and to pull together many different ideas: things he has read in a book about pirates, experiences he has had with planting, his love for geography. His enthusiasm for the continuities in nature is eclectic and expansive, and the journal provides a place where he can express that holistic attitude.

Our work in the journals continues all year. It is an activity that the children come to depend upon. The journals become records of the ways in which they are pulling their many resources as thinkers together. At some point in the year all of the children's journals will contain drawings, sketches, and diagrams illustrating their thinking. There will be poems, stories about trips, creative writing that attempts to communicate both their factual knowledge and their aesthetic response to a topic. As their teacher, I place no restrictions on what form the journals should take and what belongs in them. The children have taught me to trust their ability to develop an eclectic and flexible approach in their pursuit of knowledge.

SCIENCE TALKS

The structure for our science talks has developed with the goal of encouraging children to discuss difficult and open-ended questions that they have generated, questions that are not normally included in their prescribed science or social studies curriculum. In design, the talks complement the journals: Where the journal is an individual, introverted activity that prods each child to formulate his or her notion of what important questions and ideas might be, the talk is directed at group or collaborative thinking and requires the child to alter his or her language in order to converse with a group. Both activities leave the content to be covered in the children's hands, and both deemphasize the centrality of the teacher's role as leader.

As with the journals, children are introduced to the talks early in the year when they are asked to brainstorm questions they might have about their world. I explain to them that the questions they ask should be difficult questions they do not know the answer to, and, in fact, when a question is proposed by a child, we check to be sure that no one does know the answer. Throughout the year the questions are recorded on a chart, and we discuss one question each week in the order in which they were asked. Discussions usually last from 20 to 30 minutes. The following list is a sampling of some of the questions that have been asked over the past few years.

How did the universe begin?
How do people grow?
What makes electricity?
How did dinosaurs die?
How did people discover fire?
Why are there so many different languages?
How was nature made?
How did writing begin?
Does the universe end?
How does the earth turn?
What makes the wind?
Are dragons real?
Why is snow white?
How do bones stay together?

In its present form, the practice of science talk in our classroom richly represents what happens to talk when children are encouraged to speak collaboratively and develop ideas from their own life experience. This form developed, however, only after I had come to the painful conclusion that my role as the moderator of science discussions was limiting rather than expanding the children's thinking. Although I had always assumed that my participation in science discussions helped the children to stay on topic, I quickly learned when I began to audiotape and transcribe the discussions that while they did stay on topic, it was my topic they stayed on, rather than theirs. A comparison of a science talk from the fall term with a later talk from that same school year will elucidate this point as well as demonstrate what happens when the teacher's voice is kept to a minimum. The first excerpt is from a talk when the question asked was, "What will happen when we bury our jack-o-lantern?" It was asked by a child who wanted to bury our jack-o-lantern in dirt. (References to "Karen" in the text refer to me.)

OLLIE: Oh, Karen, Karen, I told you this before but I wanna tell the class. My friend,
TEACHER: Um hmm.

OLLIE: she has a huge, giant pumpkin outside . . . on her table, her, um, porch table, and, you see, her pumpkin has been on that table since Halloween, and it's not rotting.

SEAN: N-n- neither is one of mine rotting, and I have two . . .

OLLIE: And, and you see . . . and I think that it is because that those haven't been

SEAN: In air?

JEFF: Outside?

OLLIE: Yeah.

TEACHER: O.K., which we talked about earlier.

OLLIE: But I've got one and you see

TEACHER: O.K.

OLLIE: Remember the pumpkin that was on the step?

TEACHER: Yes.

OLLIE: It was inside but it wasn't rotting.

SEAN: But it fell down and broke.

VERA: Well, maybe it's because you see, maybe it's because this one rotted faster, because, um, maybe it's because it was opened up, it was cut.

TEACHER: Umm. So, so what about this one that wasn't cut up and it just started to rot. Remember we talked about that.

SEAN: It fell down, and blew up.

TEACHER: It didn't really . . . What do you think, Chloe?

In this text, it is clear that my purpose was to help make the children's statements relate to the buried jack-o-lantern and the experiences inside the classroom. Yet the children kept making efforts to generalize to other experiences they had had with rotting pumpkins. Ollie wants to talk about her observation of her friend's pumpkin; Sean points out that only one of his is rotting. I felt that my task was to keep focusing the children, and in some cases to do that I took on the role of refuting a child's remark, for example, Sean's remark that "it fell down and blew up," where I mistakenly took his metaphor of falling down and blowing up to mean that Sean really thought the pumpkin had fallen. In fact, what his language was describing was the physical process of decomposition that one of our pumpkins had gone through. First, it had collapsed, and then the whole mass had fermented and become, in effect, a larger mass of liquid and mold.

Only when the children's remarks were made visible to me through transcribing them did I look and see that in many cases I was missing the point of their comments and also limiting where they might go with their talk. By listening alone, I could not visualize the impact that my interventions were having. The process of painstakingly transcribing the tapes, and then looking carefully at what happened when I spoke, forced me to rethink the purposes and outcomes of my participation. I saw that I had to change my level and style of participation in the talks so that the children's ideas could move to the forefront of the discussions. When I consciously withdrew my voice from the center of the discussions and worked hard to be quiet, the talk changed both in format and in depth, as shown by the second excerpt, focusing on the question "Were dragons real?"

JUAN: The dinosaurs were not, they were not dragons, but the birds they were must be dinosaurs. The dinosaur birds they were must be dragons.

TEACHER: You think they must be dragons, the dinosaurs? Juan is saying dinosaurs must be dragons.

JUAN: The birds!

VERA: That's what I said. I said

TEACHER: The birds were?

JUAN: That the birds were.

JEFF: No they weren't.

GARY: 'Cause dragons can fly, you know.

VERA: You know, the dinosaurs might have another name, like, they might, like God might call them, uh, dragons, but we might think of them, we might call them dinosaurs.

ANDY: Or terrible lizard.

VERA: It's just like when a baby's born and then the parents die and people don't know her real name was . . . they name her name, they give her a name.

GARY: Um . . . um Andy gave me a brainstorm and Vera gives me a brainstorm. Well, Andy said dinosaur means terrible lizard

JEFF: Which it does

GARY: . . . Um . . . Vera and um, Juan said that d-, some dinosaurs are really dragons. Well, since dinosaurs are terrible lizards, dragons were terrible lizards too, weren't they?

As this text shows, my level of verbal participation had dropped considerably. Even when I tried to moderate the talk for Juan, who was just learning to speak English, I misunderstood his meaning, and he corrected me. What was most surprising to me, however, as I changed my role in the talks, was the way in which children worked together, as Gary says, giving each other brainstorms: collaborating, exploring, making connections among seemingly unrelated experiences and talking in ways that I could not recognize as being scientific.

I now know that I can assist the children early in the school year by simply modeling good listening and response behaviors, rather than moderating and directing the talks, and by having focused discussions about the kind of talk we are doing. When I value my own silence and keep my voice out of the discussion, I find that children quickly learn to talk to one another and that the language they use is remarkable in its flexibility and its resourcefulness.

The following excerpts from a science talk—titled "What Makes the Wind?"—illustrate the ways in which children develop their ideas. What is most important in the talks is not that the children get the right answer. Rather, the talk provides many examples of exploratory talk, co-construction of meaning, and elaboration of thinking, as described by Barnes (1976), and the use of personal narratives, culled from their life experience, to support the development of theory. By following the thinking of one child, Gary, throughout this discussion and examining the reactions of other children to that thinking, these characteristics can be more clearly demonstrated. Gary, who was 7 years old, quickly proposed an idea to explain how wind is made:

> You know when you're running really fast . . . I think at least a hundred people would run at the same time in the world.

This idea does not satisfy the group, and they struggle to understand him. In their struggle, they question, refute, and force him to reconsider his first idea. Andy objects:

> But Gary, you'll need like two thousand fifty million or more people to do, to make all that wind.

Gary rejoins:

> And there's over two thousand eight hundred and ninety four people in the world.

Vera states her confusion:

> Gary, I really don't get it. Really, I mean . . . how could all the people, like a hundred people run in the world all together, like how . . . ?

and finally Andy clinches his logic:

> You know how there's a lot of wind in the winter. Who jogs in the winter?

By the middle of the discussion, Gary had proposed a modification of his original idea, which was generally accepted as plausible by most of the children.

> I'm sort of on the same track, only people might jog in the wind, but millions of trucks, cars might cause the wind . . . At first, the wind is just floating in the air, right, the wind is just floating around.
> Trucks, trucks or cars or vans or something, they come really fast, right? And when this goes this way, it cuts through all those atoms, and all those atoms go "Whup! Zoom!"

His idea was later elaborated on by other children. One child proposed that the effects of pollution and the combination of air and gas might make wind: "Like if a big puff of air and gas gets all together . . . it pushes." Throughout the discussion, other ideas are proposed and argued, as, for example, the notion that rough water caused by giant fish swimming together or fighting makes wind. Children take observations from their own lives and attempt to relate them to the question at hand. They develop narratives to support their burgeoning theories, and these narratives use their own life experience as evidence.

In building the narrative, as Ricoeur says, the process of forming a plot or a convincing story line forces the children to use critical and creative thinking strategies to synthesize what might seem to be unrelated events into a plausible explanation. In this case, Gary takes his many observations about movement — people running, cars and trucks moving fast, tire swings — and with the help of other children's observations about movement, he constructs a possible narrative about what makes wind. As he does this, the other children are also surveying their past experiences to refute or support his theory; in effect they are thinking and talking together about how this question relates to their lives.

THE VALUE OF PERSONAL NARRATIVES

What emerges from these talks, however, goes beyond a search for correct or right-minded ideas. In these talks, children take over the discussions and moderate their own talk: They restate preceding ideas, modify them, extend them; they question, ask for clarification, give credit for early insights, and, when necessary, call for order. In fact, I have found that every child who is silent during the early talks begins to speak, question, and propose theories as the year progresses. In other words, the process of learning "how" to talk about thinking in this exploratory and collaborative manner occurs without my direct instructional intervention.

Rather, we talk very explicitly about the kind of talk we are using: what helps a discussion go forward, what stops it, how to enter a discussion, and how to give up the floor. In the early months of the talks, I have learned that I must model collaborative thinking with each new class so that they can see it as an important way of talking, even for a teacher. In addition, the children see me supporting ways of talking and giving voice to their thoughts that relate their personal sense of wonder about their world to their studies in school.

Thus the process of making thinking visible through oral and written narratives becomes continuous with rather than separate from the subjects we study, and it promotes an integrated view of our curriculum. Children see that their thoughts about the world should not be neatly compartmentalized into the separate disciplines of science, history, geography, or literature and that there are many ways to communicate that thinking. They realize that questions about the animal world lead naturally to considerations of human similarities and differences; that when they wonder about the beginning of languages, they must also consider the onset of writing; that a poem may best illustrate their understanding of the cycles of nature. Through the science journals and science talks, the use of personal narratives as important resources for understanding larger questions is recognized, and different ways of making sense of the world are valued. Children make tangible connections among the many subjects they study in school and, in a larger sense, relate their deep and very personal experience of the world to the process of their education.

6

Pigs Are Science

I love pets. And these are all the names. Dog cats lion.
John, age 7

So wrote John in September, as he began a long struggle to define how to relate to the task of writing in his science journal. John's work over the course of the school year represents the dilemma of those children who find no correlation between their lives and the world of science. It also clarifies how the teacher can work with children who are blocked in their work in science to develop a mutual understanding of what it means to think and write about science.

What is science? Often as teachers we make an assumption that every child who comes to school knows the meaning of this word and the reasons we study it. For children who enter school with little, if any, exposure to the language and subject matter of science, the process of talking and writing about it is often mysterious and frustrating. However, to be successful in the study of science throughout school, these children must find ways to master science discourse in its different forms. They must tap their personal stories about their world and in this way discover how science relates to their lives.

John, a very bright African-American child, encountered this struggle early in his first-grade year. He was new to our school and, because of the dangers of his former neighborhood, had not attended kindergarten regularly. His mother was simply too frightened to send him to school alone, and, with other small children at home, she was often unable to escort him herself. John was very alert and eager to be successful in first grade, but he realized quite quickly that he did not have the background knowledge that many other children had gained in kindergarten, and he did not seem to identify any part of his personal life experience with our study of science. In our science lessons, for example, when we were discussing classes of animals, John would sit in the back of the group with his head in his hands and cry silently. He was proud, and after trying unsuccessfully to volunteer ideas for our discussion, he would become frustrated by his inability to fathom the meaning of the categories we were talking about. For him, mammal, reptile, fish, and bird were indistinguishable.

Similarly in his work with science journals, John had not a clue as to where to begin. His entries throughout most of the fall, all produced with great difficulty, consisted of five or six words or short conversational entries such as this example:

November 5
Pigs are my pets, says me. Now that's the end of that.

Because he was having such trouble taking control of his journal, I began to sit down regularly with John and other children to assist him in defining what might go in the science journal. The following transcript records a conversation between John, his friend Al (the author of the dirt entry from the previous chapter), and myself. Al and John often had discussions about what went into the science journal, and Al was laboring to help him understand the process. At the time, John was writing about pigs again.

AL: Science is when you write things about something that really happened.
TEACHER: His question to you, Al, would pigs be science?
AL: It would, it would, it would. You could write about pigs.
JOHN: Pigs are science.
AL: They are, they are, they're science. But you can't just write that you like them.
JOHN: I like rap.
AL: You can't just write that you like them. You could write "pigs like to roll in the mud," like that.
TEACHER: What's the difference between just writing "I like pigs"?
JOHN: I like rap.
AL: Pigs, pigs, uh, if you just like something then that's not science. Science is um, that's the difference between liking, writing about something that you like, and um, writing about something that really happened.

In spite of Al's best efforts to explain that science was about "something that really happened," John still could not quite get Al's point. He went on to write about rap, because for John the notion of writing about something you liked remained foremost in his mind. The need for emotional investment with his subject came through quite clearly, and perhaps that was the beginning of relating science to his life, because, as can be seen from the next entries, a slight change in his thinking had taken place.

> *November 15*
> Rappers are cool. I'll tell you one. I was walking down the street calling out NIKES! The end.
> *November 29*
> When I get big, I will rap because its fun. I like rap. Rapnroll is very exciting.

John had understood that an entry had to tell about something, and so the entries began to sound more like a story. At this point, however, after seeing the last entry, my student teacher at the time told John that rap did not really belong in his science journal. John was clearly confused and disappointed, and as he got up to look for an eraser I came over and sat him back down to talk about his reasons for putting rap in his science journal. I was not sure how I felt about the appropriateness of the entry either, but my purpose in discussing it further with John was to nudge him in his own thinking and to try and be clearer about mine. When I asked John why rap was science, he said that it was "so exciting."

TEACHER: You say that it's science because it's so exciting.

JOHN: Yeah.

TEACHER: Can you talk about that, how does that make it science?

JOHN: It's so exciting. Because when you see stuff like that, um, you just want to, you just want to copy like, you just like it so much you wanna write about it so when you grow up, so when you grow up you know how to do it, and when you write about it, you can copy it over and over and over, until you get it, and then you can be on stage, so, and then, and then you'll, you'll be, you can be so proud of yourself.

TEACHER: Uh huh. So is, is science . . . does science go with being proud of yourself?

JOHN: No.

TEACHER: How can you explain . . . being proud of yourself, or how . . . I'm still not sure I understand.

JOHN: Yeah and it's so exciting! To see them, cause if if you haven't never been to one, well you can, you can go to 'em.

TEACHER: So, now, how does it make it science when it's something that's exciting?

JOHN: 'Cause rap has to be rap and it's so exciting, but sometimes . . . they have wires hooked up like record players . . . and that's electric, so, so . . . it's a very, why can't it go in the journal, my science journal?

TEACHER: Well, I'm just curious. Dan [student teacher] thinks it can't. I'm not sure that I think it can't, but I'm trying to understand. When you say rap is science, I'm just trying to understand how you think, what are you thinking. What is your brain saying to you?

JOHN: O.K. This is what I mean. Rap is so exciting because when you, when you never went to a rap concert, it's so exciting, like micro- and they're electric too. 'Cause like microphones are electric, and some microphones, they have wires hooked up to the the radio . . . they have it hooked up to, you know, the pianos and stuff and they got it plugged in, and those are electric. 'Cause that's how you write about it. . . . So can I?

TEACHER: Sure.

JOHN: But is it science?

TEACHER: That's what I want to know.

JOHN: . . . Yes!

So at this point, John established for himself that science had to be exciting, and he also expanded his ability to state what was exciting for him about rap. It was the event of the rap concert that was exciting, and in relating that event he retold his first story from his own life about something that might be science. Embedded in that story (as one might expect for a 7-year-old boy) was the realization that it was the technology that really excited him, and he clearly decided that rap was scientific.

The criteria of excitement continued for John, as he said to me in December when I asked him why he was writing about snakes, jack-o-lanterns, and dogs:

JOHN: Well, see you wrote on the board "Science Talk," and that's why I just figured out, and that was science, 'cause you said that was science.

TEACHER: So since I put it on the board and we had a science talk about our jack-o-lanterns, then you knew that it can go in there . . . but what about the snakes?

JOHN: Mean I just knew that, that's science. 'Cause if Gary can write about it in his science journal that means I can.

TEACHER: Now how did you decide that dogs were science journal stuff?

JOHN: Well, they're so exciting . . . They're animals. And mammals are science. And, and dogs are mammals.

TEACHER: Now what was on the next page? Castles. Now how did you
   decide that that was scientific?
JOHN: Because that *was* scientific! Well, I'd just copy Gary. No, he didn't
   write about castles . . . Because it's neat. And it's science, and that's
   exciting, you see, so you just wanna, I wanna write about it . . .
   'Cause see, it's just, because exciting is part of science.

As John has pointed out, he was also beginning to take his cues for
what is science from many places: from me, from his friends, and finally
from his own growing familiarity with the language of science. And John's
reflective use of the journal was helping him to clarify things that had
only been muddy before. Earlier in the year, John had been unable to
grasp our work on classes of animals, but in this conversation, the process
of writing in the journal helped him to synthesize the work he had done
earlier in our science curriculum: "And mammals are science, and dogs
are mammals." John's writing in the journal continued to expand, and it
was oriented both to his excitement about the subject and to his growing
awareness that observing the world around him and describing what he
had observed could make his entries "scientific."

> *January 24*
> Puppies are wild animals. And they act like they are getting tickled
> like babies. Well, big dogs are calm because they are old. And calm
> like I said.
> *February 14*
> Crystals sparkle and geodes are smooth to feel. At the bottom what's
> so neat about them, they sparkle a lot and they are neat, just remem-
> ber that.

Finally in late February, John settled comfortably into his work with
the journal and began a series of rich observational entries focusing on the
different animals in the classroom.

> *February 18 and March 7*
> Newts. What I like about newts is I like the way they swim, and I
> like the different colors like green and black and how they do gymnas-
> tics. What the newts are doing now . . . And I forgot and red too.
> Oh the newts, I like the way they swim. They swim neat, and I bal-
> anced a newt (referring to his attempts to weigh one of the newts).
> *April 5*
> Tadpoles. First frogs lay eggs. Then after 28 days the tadpoles hatch
> out of the jelly. They start to breathe through their gills. Then their

tails start getting shorter and shorter. And then they start to swim
like frogs, and then their tails start to grow shorter, they grow legs
and they are a frog.

Certainly John had learned a very important skill in the language of science writing, and that is how to display the things you observe. He had
learned as well what subjects science might encompass. The final example
of John's work, which follows, shows that he then made the journal his
own, in much the same way that the poetic excerpts of another child in
the previous chapter showed her ownership of the language of science.
This excerpt followed a weekend visit John made to a farm with his
family.

April 11
Farms. Farms are a good place to live. Some people think that farms
are raggedy and just because farms are very dry. It's very beautiful
and all that sweet smelling grass and those beautiful yellow and blue
flowers and the fields.

While John continued his growth in the journal, his interest in science
expanded into other subjects. He began to prefer to read books about
nature, and he wrote extensively for several weeks about the classroom
newts, producing a book for our library.

NEWTS
Sometimes when newts are sleepy they sleep very weird. They sleep
floating under water with their eyes open.

DOING ACTIVITIES
They swim with their arms back and forth and they use their tails to
help them swim. Newts love wet water.
Newts can stay underwater for fifteen minutes because I timed it.
And if you have a pet newt you should feed them pet food which will
be dried worms and tiny fish. You should feed them three times a
week.
Newts live in a pond. Sometimes when they get skinny and you can
see the newt bones, make sure your newts eat their food.

HOW TO MAKE A HOME FOR A NEWT
You should put in a tank, rocks and sticks and plants and water bugs.
You should put water half way up the tank. That's how big. Make
sure your newt does not escape because they are hard to see and you
can step on your newt and don't put a top on the tank because they
couldn't breathe the air.

What made it possible for John to arrive at an expanded understanding of science was both the process of writing in the journal and his extended conversations about it with me and with his friends, which helped him to recognize that his life and his personal stories had relevance to our study of science. In the process of convincing me that rap was science and clarifying why "exciting" had to also be part of that world, John discovered that science was laden with the same aesthetic and emotional intensity that often characterized his other interactions with the world around him. That the content of the journal was open-ended and was not dictated by a teacher allowed John to define science in his own way, to discover which of *his* stories were about science. Certainly he used many clues from his classroom environment, but essentially he placed those in his context. Ultimately, the concept of excitement and of wonder held sway for him in establishing the criteria for inclusion in his science journal.

WHAT IS SCIENCE?

My interactions with John around his science journals also began a reeducation for me as to how to think about science. Although I thought I had originally conceptualized an open-ended forum for the children's silent contemplations of the world, my picture of the science journal did not include subjects that I considered to be from other domains. When he had first started writing about rap music in his science journal, I was completely at a loss as to how to steer him in a more "correct" direction. I went home and spoke with my teenage son about John's placement of rap in his science journal. He was not at all surprised and launched into a long explanation of how rap was one of the most highly complex music genres being produced at the time. That nudged my thinking a bit but did not convince me. I somehow did not associate the idea of producing sound in a studio with writing in the science journals. Only when I interviewed John more closely about rap did he help me make the connection. John taught me to suspend disbelief as a teacher and to leave my judgment in abeyance in service of a child's development. (This is a lesson I have to relearn over and over again.) Rather than my "teaching" John what science was, we struggled together to understand his changing picture of science.

Since then, I have been nudged again and again by the children I teach. Other children like John have taught me that the word *science* is not immediately understood as representing a particular body of knowledge. These children are unlike John in that many of them are girls whose parents, though well intentioned, have not clearly identified the parts of their own lives that relate to the study of science. In some cases the children have many books about science, regularly visit museums, and take field trips. Yet when they come to school and are asked by their teacher to write, or speak, with some authority about "science," they are absolutely stymied. They have no idea what to write about. It takes a very explicit discussion about what science is to help them begin to match their personal experience with the subject we are studying. Generally I find that a discussion with myself alone is not very effective; it seems that other children are more articulate than I when they explain their understanding of science.

John's story also underscores another, larger point that I am only beginning to think about. The ways we expect children to talk, think, and write about science make a large assumption about what the language of science is and ought to be. That is, that the language of science must be formed and articulated in a particular way, using previously established vocabulary and specific cognitive structures. For example, we ask, "What is a shadow?", seeking a generalizable answer that will show that children have grasped the overall theoretical point. The children reply, "A shadow is like night lying down" or "It's part of darkness" or "Day is night time for the shadow. I mean, not really, but that's what it's like cause the person blocks the light." They speak and write metaphorically or in terms of the particular. The form of *their* language of science does not originally parrot the forms that we believe indicate real mastery of that subject matter.

However, as I confront the different forms that children use, and struggle with my own need to somehow improve their use of terms and the ways that they process and interpret information, I wonder if the ways that science is spoken and written about, ways that were established by a small and elite portion of Western society, reflect more an elitist discourse than a natural mode of communicating about the world of science. If we look at the vast numbers of people that have historically been excluded from scientific discussions, and that includes the majority of the population in this country, one might wonder why they are excluded. I would propose that it is because they were unable to utilize correctly and appropriately the very precise language of science; thus, they were left out of the conversation.

As a teacher, my growing discomfort with the lines that are drawn between colloquial language and the language of science, between children's stories about their observations of nature and the objective descriptions required in most science discussions, arises from the fact that over time many of the children I teach may eventually be excluded from those conversations by virtue of the fact that they cannot say what they know in the correct terms! I know that these children are bright, curious, and filled with closely observed knowledge. Like John, they find the natural world "exciting." Excitement, wonder, and awe characterize their interactions with hands-on science.

John and other children have made me consider that the object of teaching science is not to teach the correct usage and application of scientific concepts and terminology, but rather to engage as many children as possible in observing, experimenting, talking, and writing about the world. That process must begin with their deep emotional attachments and focus, as children naturally do, on the surprises in nature. As Fox-Keller (1983) points out in her biography of scientist Barbara McClintock, a Nobel Prize winner in maize genetics, "reason and experiment, generally claimed to be the principle means of this pursuit, do not suffice" (p. 201). She describes how McClintock's work was framed by her "feeling for the organism" and how the process of careful observation and creative insight enabled her to "see further and deeper into the mysteries of genetics" (p. 197). For children, a "feeling for the organism" is ever-present and easily elicited. That awareness can be a starting point from which conversations about science begin. I believe that those conversations must be held on the child's terms. As a teacher, my role is one of exploring children's meanings and learning to speak in their dialects so that our discussions about science are ongoing, continuing from one day to the next, and gradually expanding in depth and understanding.

The conversations we have had through the medium of the science journal have continued to teach me that as an adult my conceptualization of science is too narrow: Science means *all* sciences, not just the natural or physical sciences. Science means all ways of being, not just present ways of being. When I look at the writing being done over the years, I see that the children's entries reflect thinking about sociology, anthropology, archaeology, religion, philosophy, paleontology, linguistics, creativity, and many other fields. They are not prepared to limit their thinking about the world in any way. And now, neither am I. As Tony writes so succinctly:

> Does the universe end? I don't think so. Because what would be at the end?

I have learned to wait and see how each child will shape the journal and in what ways they will join their understanding of the world to their writing about science. John and others continue to show me that anticipating the end result of children's thinking is like believing the universe is bounded. Each child's journey as a thinker moves outward in ways I cannot anticipate and should not limit.

7

Rainbows on the Floor

TEACHER: How are colors made in nature? . . . Why are apples green from some trees, red from others? Why are carrots orange and why are roses red?

JIANA: It um, um, like um . . . Karen did with the um, eggs, like s-squirt that um, color stuff stuff in.

TEACHER: Mmhmm.

JIANA: It could be um, like, like rain, like makin' like different colors and rain can be goin' in those seeds because sometime when it rains, there, there are rainbows on the floor.

I am sitting on the floor, wedged between Donald on my right and Jiana on my left. Jiana has just proposed a theory about what makes different colors in nature to the 20 other first graders sitting in a circle with us. The children furrow their brows in an effort to follow her thought. Some are not even looking at her. One child enters the discussion:

DONALD: Well it might be how, like it might be how uh, like if it takes time, like if someone t-, puts um, wa-, waters a tree, like this time, and then, they water at the same time the next day, it might have, mi-, it might like get, um different colors because i-its different times like, like a red apple might be, like when someone um, waters a tree very early, or maybe, maybe it depends on um . . . like how, how many times the rain does . . .

"Jiana," I whisper. "Listen, they are talking about your idea." Jiana looks at me, then at Donald, then gets "goofy," as I call it, rolling her eyes and pretending to fall over backwards. The other children continue to build on Jiana's idea.

SHELLY: You know it could be, things that grow on trees may get like, water from the trees, and the sugar that comes, that's down . . . and the things that grow in the ground, probably, probably ha-, get the water, and the like . . . the soil from the ground, and, that's maybe how they get *a* color.

ROBIN: Pumpkins don't grow from trees.

SHELLY: Well, um, I know.

ROBIN: They grow from the garden.

SHELLY: But I was saying that, maybe, you know whatever it grows on, that was just, an example.

SARAH: Well, you see, it could be from the rain. It could be, also from the rain because, the rain keeps recycling because . . . because um, do you know, really, the r- . . . you know the rain that rains on us right now, it could be a hundred years old . . .

I could not have anticipated, when I first met Jiana, that she would ever be able to participate in a science talk. My picture of her as a thinker was bounded by her inability to express herself coherently in a way that I could follow. I naturally interpreted that limitation as reflecting a deficit in thinking, one that could not help but inhibit her participation in talking about difficult science questions.

Science talks, however, have a way of throwing any teacher off his or her horse. Often what we think will happen during a talk and what really happens are completely unrelated. Since I began collecting data on science talks, my understanding of children's oral language has evolved considerably. Now I know that in order to follow the talks I must bring to them the child's mind and I must watch and listen carefully for clues as to when an idea is making sense. That can be done, as I learned early on, only if I am quiet. Silence has enabled me to hear the sense that children are making, and that sense is much more complex than I had first realized.

As I began to see the complexity of the talks, I expanded my inquiry to include a consideration of how children use more complex language, particularly metaphor and analogy, to further their thinking. I hope in this chapter to convey the ways in which I have begun to make further sense of the abstract and expressive thinking skills that children naturally bring to their study of science, ways that can assist teachers in exploiting children's natural abilities as thinkers and learners.

THE POWER OF METAPHOR

In speaking of the congruence between the use of metaphor and the development of narrative, Ricoeur (1984) notes that although metaphor is a "figure of discourse" and narrative is a genre, "the meaning-effects produced by each of them belong to the same basic phenomenon of semantic innovation" (p. ix). Metaphor takes seemingly unrelated and possibly "incompatible" phenomena and produces a new semantic relationship through their juxtaposition. Narrative synthesizes diverse and separate actions, characters, and events into a plot. "In both cases, the new thing — the as yet unsaid, the unwritten — spring up in language" (Ricoeur, 1984, p. ix).

Thus, in the process of building her theory, Jiana used a metaphor that was embedded in her brief narrative to reconcile unrelated images and events. The incident of egg dyeing, which she had participated in a few days earlier, was specifically used to illustrate, or point to, an idea. At the time she obviously did not say, "Oh, so that's how colors get in apples." But in the framework of building a narrative that addressed a specific question, Jiana used her first experience with egg dyeing and coupled it with her observation of oil spills on city streets ("rainbows on the floor") to make an attempt to develop a theory. Her thinking process clearly is one of semantic innovation and represents what Ricoeur (1984) calls "this power of the metaphorical utterance to redescribe a reality inaccessible to direct description" (p. xi.). He sees this use of poetic language as a means by which the individual can speak about issues of being in the world that are indescribable except through the process of crossing the boundaries of the normal and everyday use of language.

In their collaborative talk, I have repeatedly observed children using narratives to build scientific theories. In the early stages of the science talks, these narratives were very difficult for me to follow and often led me to believe that the children were not making any sense. However, I noticed in the midst of my confusion that they did not seem to have any trouble following one another's train of thought. For example, the following text came in a discussion focused on the question, "Why is it summer when the sun is farther away from the world, and winter when the sun is closer?"

VERA: . . . like the North Pole where Santa lives . . . he, then Santa doesn't get any sun.

SEAN: That is true.

TEACHER: Is that all year round Santa doesn't get any sun, or is there a time when Santa gets a lot of sun?

VERA: Well, he gets some sun, but he never gets a lot.

SEAN: Down below it only gets a little sun.

GARY: And that's how the middle is so hot.

TEACHER: Why?

GARY: 'Cause on the bottom, the the the world goes around the sun so when the sides are a little warm, the top isn't cold, so the middle has to be hot.

VERA: The middle, the middle's the closest to the sun 'cause the sides aren't as close, like this is the sun *(using her hands for a model)*. Now the sides go a little bit off . . . This is the sun, right? Now this is the earth. Now listen, it's spinning around like this so only this part and this part and the like, the sun is going right for here *(pointing to the middle of her fist), and part of the sun is, it's like it's breaking up and it's going like, like Peter Pan says, he says the first shadow broke into a thousand pieces.* It's like that, 'cause *like the sun's breaking up.* It's like parts of it, part of the sun's going to this part, a little bit of the sun's going to this part, and most of the sun is going to this part.

This text is particularly striking because it shows three characteristics of science talking that 6- and 7-year-olds regularly demonstrate: using narrative, or storytelling, talk to develop an idea; personifying to illustrate a point; and developing a metaphor or analogy to make the intellectual leap toward theory. For example, early in the text Vera refers to Santa in the North Pole and seriously uses that reference to develop a story about where the sun might not reach. Later she says the sun is "breaking up," and in alluding to the literary reference of Peter Pan, she develops a very poetic metaphor to illustrate the idea of how sunlight might, in fact, break up as it hits the earth.

Hillman (1975) describes personification as "a way of being in the world and experiencing the world as a psychological field, where persons are given with events, so that events are experiences that touch us, move us, appeal to us" (p. 12). He characterizes the process as one that helps us to "understand," rather than "explain" (p. 15), and that "shifts the discussion from nominalism to imagination, from head to heart" (p. 14). Thus Vera easily uses referents such as Santa Claus and Peter Pan to give life to her story about science, in effect anchoring her thinking about an abstract idea to her feeling about the world.

Leacock (1972) describes the power of metaphor as a tool for abstract thinking. She notes that "through the metaphor, the relevant characteristics of a situation are abstracted and stated in the form of an analogy that clearly divests it of extraneous features" (p. 129). Because metaphor generally pulls an image from one context and places it in a new, and seemingly opposed reference, it abbreviates the connecting ideas from the first idea to the last and, as such, requires the listener to make some leaps of thought. Rothenberg (1979), in describing how scientific thinking uses metaphoric thought to develop new theories, labels this process "Janusian thinking," using the reference to the Roman god Janus to illustrate how metaphoric thinking requires the thinker to reconcile two opposite ideas into a unified image. Vera's use of the image of shadows breaking up to talk about sunlight hitting the earth represents the practice of Janusian thinking in action. Her image of the sun breaking up is related to a shadow breaking up, thus juxtaposing two opposite phenomena to illustrate a point. Although Vera's language is presented in a way that I often find difficult to follow, it is perfectly intelligible to her peers. Difficult ideas gain clarity through the development of the narrative, and metaphors are the bridge to the theory.

From the narratives that I have heard used in science talks, I have concluded that children, even disadvantaged urban children, observe the natural world very carefully and mark certain observations with an invisible exclamation point, as it were. If the opportunity arises, many of these marked observations are then brought into play as potential symbolic representations of an idea. Often, however, adults mistake the child's symbolic representations as immature conceptualizations of an idea. In other words, Vera's reference to Santa Claus or Peter Pan in the midst of a science discussion would throw a distractor into the adult's thought pattern. When I hear the words *Santa Claus*, I immediately discount the statements to follow because the narrative has not followed the rules of theoretical science discourse. My stance as a listener changes from one of listening to one of evaluating. How can one take an idea about the sun's energy breaking up seriously, when in the next breath the child is using Peter Pan to complete the thought? Donaldson (1978) proposes that in some ways it may be the adults, not the children, who need to decenter their thinking. Adults are often easily diverted because their thinking proceeds hierarchically, rather than radiationally. What we consider to be quaint examples of the child's imaginative thought might more often be metaphoric attempts to build theories about how the world works.

ANALYSIS OF A SCIENCE TALK: HOW DID NATURE BEGIN?

An examination of the text of one science talk will further illustrate both the process of collaborative thinking and the metaphoric language that children often use to express their ideas. This talk occurred in the spring of 1991. It opened with Robin, who made an attempt to identify the parameters of what they were considering. (Each dot indicates a one-second pause.)

ROBIN: . . . . . . Nature was made, um, like with dirt and . . and seeds
. . also um . . . wi- . . . and the uh . . sun.
SHELLY: Well, how were, how was the sun made? How was dirt made?
How was o- how was oceans made?

FRANNY: So, Robin, that couldn't be, 'cause if we're talking about how nature was made it has to be like . . . how nature *was* made, you know?

DONALD: Yeah, like

FRANNY: 'Cause

ROBIN: Yeah, but, but

BRANDY: I think um, that um, nature was made like, from a like a seed like that was just like, under dirt, and then like, maybe um . . . like roots started like coming, and then it, they dropped more seeds and then, um, all that plants came.

ROBIN: Maybe.

DONALD: Maybe it was because, maybe . . . . . Um. Maybe, you know, you know how, when like, um, how the leaves, kind of um . . um, you know how there was plants way long ago? For dinosaurs to eat? Well maybe the leaves fell off, sometimes and and they and they went, and they went deep into the ground, and you know the stems? The other part rotted and the stems, and they started to grow nature.

The other children immediately pushed to define the parameters of the talk further. At first they used very tentative language to propose more ideas, and they started with what they themselves had observed in their world. The talks at this point are what Barnes (1976) labels "exploratory." They sound messy, that is, the children use their language to grope around collectively for an idea that holds up to scrutiny, often returning to an early idea and working with it to refine it.

BRANDY: I know Robin, but um, like h-how, like if . . . how is the dirt, like, made?

JIANA: Yeah, but maybe that when the seeds drop . . . the um the um . . the dirt started to grow when when they put the um, seeds in the um, under the ground.

ROBIN: But maybe

FRANNY: Robin, Robin, maybe the dirt was, I kind of agree with Robin, because maybe the dirt was made before the plants!

DONALD: I know that has to be, because i-, plants can't grow without dirt.

SHELLY: Right.

BRANDY: Yeah, and seeds can't fall without trees.

TEACHER: So maybe we should go back even farther to the dirt.

JOEL: That's true . . .

ROBIN: Yeah but, you know how someone

JOEL: To the dirt or mud.

ROBIN: Someone doesn't always talk about *something* first?

TEACHER: Yeah.

ROBIN: Maybe I wasn't talking about that first, maybe I was talking about the plants first.

In this case the children returned to Robin's initial proposal that it started with dirt, and they reason that dirt came before seeds, and seeds came before plants. Their attempts to work logically from one idea to the next, reducing the possible answers, is consistent in the early stages of the talks. Throughout the talks, the children think collaboratively, often building on one another's ideas in piggyback fashion. To the adult listener, the trains of thought are often difficult to follow and give the impression that the talk is going nowhere.

In the midst of the progression of ideas, children often comment on their own thinking process, hoping it will clarify why they made a statement. Robin pointed out to her friends that she had had the idea about the dirt early but could not explain it right away: "You know how someone doesn't always talk about something first." In other words, it takes awhile to get to the point you start with. Her comment here is typical of the kind of talking about thinking that occurs in the science talks along with the talk about the content of the science talks.

The talks, which last from 20 to 30 minutes, often proceed in fits and starts. Generally in the middle there is a lull, and the children appear to be befuddled. They seem to pause, regroup, and then one child will move forward. In this talk, Franny took up the question once again of how far back in time they were looking.

FRANNY: When the dinosaurs were made, um, in a book it showed that there were plants so we have to go further back before the dinosaurs.

SARAH: If we wanna do plants. You could go like, um, when dinosaurs were, or you could go, you know, real far back.

JOEL: Past dinosaurs i- there were, there were, sharks were alive, they were.

TEACHER: O.K. So back even further than that.

FRANNY: Well, then, I have an idea because if we went way, way, way back, then, then, we couldn't say that there was no grass and

TEACHER: Was there ever a time, you think, when there was no grass?

FRANNY: I know . . . But then, if there was no grass, there might not be any water, so of course plants couldn't grow. There might not be any water if, because the plants need water to grow.

So Franny reduced the time frame back to a period when there was no water. Her logic caused the group to explode with excitement, and disorder broke out even among the teachers.

SHELLY: Franny you're right! So it coulda been that it's too hot. That water started nature!
STUDENT TEACHER: Water that started nature?
SHELLY: You know
DONALD: There couldn't because
SHELLY: because
TEACHER: Wait, wait, wait, wait, wait, wait, wait, wait, wait! I'm getting confused.
FRANNY: Like we can't grow without water, and
SARAH: We can't live without water.
SHELLY: Plants can't live without water.
ANDY: I can't live without it.
DONALD: Monkeys, monkeys can't live without water!

Once the excitement subsided, the children tried to figure out how "nature" might have started in the water. Joel proposed "that plants live in the water, so way back, there were plants in the ocean." Franny had continued to wonder about how the plants got in the ocean, and she reintroduced the problem of the seed into the discussion: "Anyways if there were [plants], the oceans might not be able to get up to the plants so they can grow, and also, how would the seeds be in there because there were no seeds then." A few minutes later, Robin returns to Franny's problem of the seeds:

ROBIN: Maybe um, the um . . . um way way way way way way way way way way
TEACHER: Millions of years?
ROBIN: Yeah before the dinosaurs were alive, there was no water . . . .
   Maybe the um, nature was made with uh, little, little seeds, very little, and people couldn't see them. Well, I mean, well, there were no people um,
JOEL: But they're so small that people couldn't see them.
ROBIN: and then, um, it started to make a earth, and then, um . . . . well, I don't mean one seed, I mean lots of seeds
FRANNY: But there could, there couldn't be seeds made then.
BRANDY: I know, but Robin, that was what I said.

The children found this idea to be very dissonant, and they refuted her very strongly. Robin's metaphor, in which the symbol of the seed represents the beginning of life, is incompatible with their picture of the seed as something that grows in dirt. Brandy reminds her that she mentioned seeds earlier in the discussion. Robin persists saying, "but people have different ideas," and she makes a great effort to restate her idea. "I mean that there were lots and lots of little little seeds, and then they started to get bigger and bigger and then it started to go together and make a big earth." She seems to be trying to explain an image she has of seeds combining to create the diversity on earth. The children still object, and Robin tries again:

ROBIN: I don't mean that there were, there were like, people, then. Maybe there were like, little, whatever things in them, and then they were, then they started to come together and then they got, and then it got bigger and bigger and bigger . . .
SHELLY: What do you mean? What do you mean "little things"? 'Cause we don't really get any idea when you say there were little things.
ROBIN: Well, but I don't know the word.
SHELLY: Well, make one up!

Shortly thereafter the discussion ended, but the talk about beginnings continued with this class for weeks afterward. Robin's use of the "seed" as a symbol for something that might have started life in water was hotly debated, and the children began to look for books that discussed the earliest times on earth. Eventually we read *Life Story* by Virginia Burton (1962). The book confirmed in a very clear and simple way for the children that their thinking was close to the way scientists viewed the beginnings of life on earth, and they were certainly amazed at themselves.

I have found as I have participated in these science talks that I am also continuously amazed at the powerful and insightful thinking of which 6- and 7-year-olds are capable. As they gain confidence in their abilities to "co-construct meanings" (Barnes, 1976), they grow more tenacious in their desire to follow muddy ideas through to the end. Their identities as thinkers expand to include the right to name the world in new ways—as Shelly said when Robin did not know the word, "Make it up!"—and they begin to construct new theories, some of which are unnervingly close to the theories being proposed by scientists today.

WHO HAS THE AUTHORITY TO SPEAK ABOUT SCIENCE?

As the talks have become more embedded in my curriculum, the children have moved on to interpret the purpose of the talks more broadly than I intended. As with the subject matter of science journals, the questions have moved from strictly science questions into the domain of ontological questions. For example, the following questions were part of a recent class list.

Will the earth survive?
Why are there so many different languages?
How did writing begin?
How did people change from apes to humans?
Does the universe end?

Children, at 6 and 7 years of age, want to talk about being in the world, and in the process of expanding the talks to include any big question, they engage in discussions about how one comes to know the answer to any question and how that answer is verified.

I witnessed one such discussion in February of 1991, when the children were considering the question, "How did the dinosaurs die?" I had thought this would be a fairly straightforward discussion because, even though everyone admitted they did not know the final answer, they all agreed that they probably knew most of the recent theories from scientists. However, they decided to discuss the question because "no one knew the real answer," and that initial orientation to the question of knowing set the stage for a remarkable group effort to think about what knowledge is.

In the process of this discussion, the children stated and agreed that scientists do not know all the answers: "Just because a scientist says it's so doesn't mean it is, because how do they know everything that ever happened?" They also thought that there might be many explanations for why the dinosaurs died: "It doesn't have to be just one idea because how can we say only one thing happened? It could be many different things." Many children spoke about how books did not necessarily "say the truth," and they agreed that people should study "the places dinosaurs lived by where we find the bones and see if they had the right food, or if there was too much heat."

As the weeks passed, this group of children turned increasingly to talking about the question of epistemology. In April, they took up the question "Does the universe end?" and early parts of the talk were focused on what the question really meant:

SARAH: [who had asked the question] I'm just asking the question. I don't know.

DONALD: Do you mean, um, like, will it like be gone some day, or do you mean, does it go on out in space all the way?

Later, Donald continued, "because the universe is like, what people think, because you've gotta know what 'the universe' means to answer that question." Sarah agreed that it was a difficult question to answer "in a way that people could understand." In other words, the language of explanation was too complex.

Much of the discussion proceeded on the level of knowing when something has ended. If you do not know that the universe has ended, has it ended? "If we're in the graveyard, and the world ends, we're gonna be with it but we're not gonna know it." The vastness of the question produced many layers of thinking:

DONALD: The universe is everything that can be thought or that is here right now.
WILLIAM: Donald, I think the universe is space. Like I'm not the universe, this table isn't the universe . . . It's out in the universe.
BRANDY: But there's, there might not be only one universe, there might be a couple.

It is often the case, as I listen to young children talk, that I am in awe of their capabilities as thinkers. What confounds me is how children of this age can often devise explanations for difficult questions that are very close to theories currently accepted by the scientific community, theories that they would not have had access to in the resources available to them. Through this process of thinking together and using their natural ability to make connections, children show remarkable tenacity and creativity as thinkers; they are willing to grapple with the most difficult ideas, and they have no difficulty "decentering" in the midst of a discussion. That is, their flexibility as thinkers enables them to work with many ideas at one time, and they constantly attempt to build stories and images that allow those ideas to be synthesized into a coherent theory.

Rothenberg's (1979) study of creativity in science illustrates how key ideas have resulted from a thinking process that uses the "leap of thought" to synthesize thinking. When scientists use metaphoric thinking, it is usually a personal and internal language that is not represented in the final description of the idea itself. No one is required to follow the path of that thinking to understand the idea. Yet this process is integral to the practice of science. It is one of the ways of talking science that Lemke (1990), Britton (1990), and Barnes (1976) suggest children need to engage in to develop science concepts. But when children, who seem to have a natural inclination to work through difficult ideas using a storymaking process, use this kind of language to explain themselves, many adults find it difficult, if not impossible, to follow them and so discount the ideas embedded within the narrative.

Because most teachers of science, like myself (and I characterize teachers broadly here to include teachers from kindergarten through graduate education), have not experienced this kind of talk in the context of our own education, we rarely recognize it as a particular form of science discourse that should be encouraged and maintained throughout the child's experience as a student of science. And so at some point in the process of studying science, this natural gift for metaphoric thinking, this way of conceptualizing the world in narrative, is silenced and remains untapped as a powerful force in thinking and learning. If, however, we begin to reclaim our sense of wonder and unimpeded thinking, we also develop the ability to follow the leaps of thought that children so easily make. One is left to ponder what powerful understandings our children might achieve if their natural abilities as creative and critical thinkers were encouraged and exploited rather than contained and redirected in the interests of what we incorrectly perceive to be real science.

PART III
Art as Story

Spring is a leaf born
some flowers bloom
animals awake
people start to play
Violet comes back to the school.
Tian, age 6

There is an aura of excitement that rises above a classroom where children are engaged intensely in artistic activity. Perhaps it comes from the series of surprises that children continuously present in their art: surprises that sometimes revolve around aesthetics, a bold burst of color and form that jumps off a page; surprises about ways of being, when my vision of a child like Tian is suddenly transformed by his poem; surprises of instruction, when a child singing out loud and out of turn somehow transports us all to another level of understanding. There is an aura of excitement in the classroom engaged in the arts, and also one of serious intent. Children who know that their artistic expressions are valued take their work as artists seriously. They know what I, as a student, never did, and that is that the arts are transformative: What you know and what you create from that knowledge changes you and changes everyone around you. It makes you powerful and gives you authority within that community. It enables you to feel some control over your history as a learner.

How do teachers offer all children expanded opportunities for communicating about their learning? This section takes the uses of narrative in the classroom to another level, discussing the ways in which the arts — drawing, painting, movement and dance, drama, poetry, music, and creative writing — enable children to think about new knowledge in more complex and meaningful ways by transforming their understanding of difficult concepts into metaphoric language and acts. It does not present the use of the arts in a disembodied fashion that relegates art instruction in the classroom to a series of lessons on media or technique, along with weekly discussions of great works of art. Rather, media, technique, and art history merge with an understanding of the dynamics of the creative process to offer children broad avenues for expression and understanding.

I did not come to this work with the arts with any experience or training as a visual artist, a performer, or a creative writer. My earliest work with the arts was grounded in very simple uses of paint and clay, simple songs, and dramatic play. Those were the tools I used to expand the expressive activities available to the children I taught. What I began to see were the surprises: the ways that children could learn to read through their artworks; the potential for communication that painting offered a nonverbal child; the joy that artistic activity brought to children and teachers alike. Those things seemed important, and, like my early belief that informal talk needed to be a part of my classroom, ongoing art activity became critical to the happiness and well-being of both myself and the children I taught.

Over time, I saw more. There were the children who, by any standard, were failures in school but produced powerful works of art that somehow defied mainstream assumptions about their potential as thinkers. There were the dramas, poems, and paintings that told stories, sometimes wonderful, sometimes painful. Finally, there was the realization that all children could think more deeply and push the boundaries of their own learning through the arts — that the arts offered a new definition of the language of learning.

Too often, when we think about appropriate ways to communicate what we know in schools, we think only of oral and written language. Even those children who are fluent speakers and writers, though they will be successful within those standards, are confined by that limitation. I now know, as Bakhtin (1986) points out, "if the word 'text' is understood in the broad sense — as any coherent complex of signs — then even the study of art . . . deals with texts" (p. 103). For children who are new English speakers, and for the many children who are struggling to learn what the discourse of school is, a broad definition of how one communicates about learning, how one creates "texts" about the world, enables them to participate more fully in conversations about knowledge. As teachers recognize that children can communicate what they understand through pictures, dances, songs, poems, and dramas, these products of the learning process offer them a more complete picture of the children they teach.

Further, conversations about learning, when focused on the arts, enable children and teachers to speak together in new ways about content, forms of expression, communication, and excellence. Bakhtin's notion of understanding intentionality in language can easily be extended to include all forms of expression. Just as speaker and listener work to build a common ground from which to speak to one another, so artists and audience work to establish common understandings. Those understandings require negotiations around point of view and intentionality: The artist's intent is met with the audience's interpretation. When teachers and children begin to speak about learning through the arts, they initiate new kinds of conversations, some of which may not even rely on the spoken word. Regarding a work of art becomes much more than seeing it and walking away. Rather, it provides an opportunity for everyone to create new worlds, new texts, and new kinds of stories; to acknowledge that there are different ways of understanding the world and a variety of forms that expression can take.

The chapters in this section describe how the process of integrating the arts into the curriculum changes both what we study in schools and how we study it. The relationship between children's use of stories and their work as artists and thinkers is presented through descriptions of how the arts help both children and their teachers to build more complete pictures of the teaching and learning process. Chapter 8 introduces the potential of the art experience as a vehicle for learning and proposes that teachers and children are epistemologists working in a cooperative venture. It documents the ways in which art experiences, like science talks, have helped me to better understand what my students know and want to know, and it illustrates the kinds of surprises that intense involvement in the arts brings to the classroom. Chapter 9 continues the exploration of epistemology as an important exercise that is furthered through the artistic process and offers a description of how a specific unit of study in science developed around the creative arts.

8

The Flexible Mind of Childhood

I have always believed that an event has not happened until it has passed through the mind of a creative artist able to explain its significance. I suppose that is why from the earliest times we have had the narrators who sat around the campfires at night to recount the heroic adventures of that day.

James Michener (1977)

In our culture, we have always relegated the role of artist to a few people, assuming, I think, that real artistic activity only happens for those who possess "talent" and that most of us lack that mysterious ingredient. We look to those who decide to pursue a life in the arts as the enigmatic inheritors of talent: We search their childhood, their parentage, their lifestyle and point to those as proof that the capacity to live in the arts is reserved for those with special gifts. Few of us include ourselves in that world, and there is a general conviction about artists that mirrors how we view saints, shamans, and witch doctors. They have some kind of special sight, and in thinking about the world, they often speak in tongues — conveying insights that are important, and, often, elusive.

We also know, however, that many artists look to childhood as that time when artistic expression is at its most pure and direct level and that they often strive to regain the simplicity and clarity that young children's expressions naturally convey. Yet for most adults, children's art and expressions are often mistakenly viewed, as I have pointed out in earlier chapters, as naive, magical, constraining, and misconceived; and because of those assumptions, they are excluded from serious discussions about teaching and learning. The separation of art from life, then, is a process that often begins when children enter school. And for most children, that separation represents a loss in expressive opportunities at a time of maximum learning potential when they most need to expand, rather than limit, their communication strategies. I do not believe that the process of separation is a natural, adaptive occurrence for most children, and further, I do not believe that artistic and creative vision is naturally restricted to a small minority of unique adults.

This chapter begins a discussion of what happens when the art experience is placed at the center of the curriculum and fills a number of roles: (1) *the arts as representing a methodology for acquiring knowledge*; (2) *the arts as subject matter for study, in and of themselves*; and (3) the arts as an array of expressive opportunities for communicating with others, or *art as story*. What I have found over the years is that in all of these functions, the arts become a way of thinking about thinking, and I believe that this way is very natural and accessible to children. The process and dynamics of the art experience best capture the way children make their world sensible from very early years on. What is unfortunate in American education, however, is that as soon as children enter school they are gradually taught that their natural way of understanding the world is not an important and valid way; that part of the process of being educated is to exclude and isolate their most powerful means of making the world sensible and to adopt a more linear language style in which logic prevails, a style that represents almost exclusively a hierarchical, convergent, "scientific" way of ordering the world.

I believe that part of that process of persuasion occurs because teachers, in their training, are taught that thinking becomes more sophisticated and advanced as it conforms more and more to a language-based communication system. As soon as children enter school, we want them to use language in particular ways to acquire and communicate about knowledge. We use textbooks, objective tests, charts, and workbooks to introduce and assess ideas. We overload children with words and words and words about every conceivable subject, and these words represent the limited communication structure of the adult world. They do not even slightly acknowledge the more expansive system of expression, communication, and problem solving that children possess when they begin school.

In contrast to this, however, our understanding of thinking has been expanded over the years, and we now generally agree that the creative process is an integral part of higher-level thinking. If one looks carefully at the most important achievements in science in the past, for example, creative thinking was integral to those achievements. The personal accounts of Einstein, Darwin, and McClintock in maize genetics, all relate a creative process in which intuition, imagination, metaphor, and visualization enabled them to gain new and important insights (Fox-Keller, 1983; Rothenberg, 1979). So in this sense I think it is safe to say that higher-level thinking cannot occur without the presence of creative thinking in partnership with critical thinking. And this is the kind of thinking that I believe most teachers hope their children will achieve.

Yet the process of reaching that goal through traditional means is, in my opinion, inherently flawed. How is it flawed? It is flawed in that we discount the natural expressive and intellectual tendencies of children to think divergently rather than convergently. It is flawed in that we limit the expressive modalities that children can use to study about, and communicate, their understanding of the world. It is flawed in that we relegate metaphoric, transformative action and talk to the world of play and exclude it from the serious pursuit of learning.

MAKING CONNECTIONS BETWEEN
THE ARTS AND SCIENCE

As a teacher-researcher, I have only recently come to see the connections between children's work in the arts and their divergent use of language in other learning contexts. For the first three years of collecting data on science talks, I thought that work was separate from my work on the arts and learning. But then a funny thing happened after I had listened to the tapes of many, many science talks and looked at the transcriptions of those talks. I realized that the children were doing with the talk what they did with their art. They were tapping a very powerful and, I believe, natural ability to think about difficult ideas through metaphoric and analogic language, and this kind of thinking directly mirrored what I had seen children doing when they used the arts to work through very difficult ideas. This metaphoric thinking, as I described in an earlier chapter, was usually embedded in long narratives that used a story to explicate a difficult idea. The imagery in the narratives was often so powerful that I must have been dense not to have seen the relationship between this kind of talk and their work as artists. However, as I saw the links between the children's work in the arts and their use of language in science talks, I began to believe that the untapped potential of metaphor ran throughout all of their attempts to understand the world and that the arts, especially, because of the freedom they offer from the restrictions of spoken language, afford teachers a very broad opportunity for studying, with children, what kinds of understandings they were building in the classroom.

I see the process of looking at these understandings as a daily exercise in epistemology, because it seems to me that epistemology is what teachers and children think about every day. I believe that for many teachers, it is one of the original reasons they go into the field. They are interested in knowledge, and they want to help children become interested in knowledge, too. More than that, though, they are naturally intrigued by the uniqueness of children's thinking, by those things that most people find "cute" about how children manifest their understanding of the world. And in point of fact and practice, teaching is a profession in which teachers study and worry over children's knowledge every single day. Now I am not saying that the ways we study it are always effective, but at a basic level that is what we do.

In the same way, children, as soon as they walk into the classroom, look around and try to size up what they do and do not know. They compare themselves to everyone else. They agonize over the fact that they cannot read, or that they do not understand multiplication, or calculus, or chemistry, or that they cannot draw a circle. They watch the teacher carefully for clues as to what he or she thinks about what they know. They ask their friends, "Am I doing this right?" As soon as any of us walks into a classroom as a student, we begin to worry about what we do or do not know, how we are going to find out what to know, and whether, when we think we know it, we are right.

Teachers and children are epistemologists, and, moreover, this is a cooperative venture. As a teacher, I need to study children's knowledge with them in many different ways and on many different levels. Although it is easy to assess children's knowledge on the most superficial levels, assessing higher-level thinking is more difficult. That kind of learning is not easily measured, and it is more difficult to encourage. I need to provide ways for children to express the metaphoric transformations that they are clearly capable of making by offering them many expanded opportunities for expressive action: to talk, paint, dance, write, build, and study together. In that way, as I allow and encourage children to reconstruct the concepts and ideas being presented in the curriculum, the children in turn learn to make their connections more explicit. Through the arts, teachers and children build an understanding together of how school concepts relate to the child's personal reality.

But let me also point out that this process is full of uncertainty. Teachers who are committed to the importance of the creative process must live with a certain amount of ambiguity and tension, with disequilibrium in the Piagetan sense. Sometimes the end result of a study is unknown and unanticipated, and the path toward that result is unclear. Teachers and children involved in learning through the arts often share this uncertainty, but they can learn to live with, and even appreciate, the place of tension and ambiguity in the learning process. Let me give an example of what I mean.

DEVELOPING A CREATIVE ARTS CURRICULUM

In late December of 1990, my first graders began a study of early humans, a study I would never have planned for children this age—but this class had a consuming interest in the origin of things, and I felt compelled to pursue the subject with them. Naturally, most of our study had to focus on books, and we literally pored over the resources available to us, reading one book, *Early Humans* (Merriman, 1989) page by page, two pages a day, scrutinizing the pictures and deciphering the small print. My problem as a teacher was how to make this topic live for these children, and also how to assess what kind of learning was taking place.

On one particular occasion, we had been talking about how fire might have been discovered. I asked the children to work in small groups to develop a theory about the discovery of fire and then to put their theory into a performance or dramatic enactment. My hope in this was that the process of movement and drama would help the children work through the problem (which seems to me inherent in studying prehistoric and historic events) of not living in that time and place, of not being able to locate themselves in the story they were being told. I wanted them to retell the story through their own actions. Small-group work in my classroom, when focusing on the dramatic arts, usually involves the children in developing and then performing their response to a problem I have presented. The rest of the class and I watch, and then there is a response time in which we ask for clarification or support parts of the group's performance. The small groups then reconvene, rerehearse, and perform a second time. The field notes that follow were written as I observed the second performance of Derek's group, focusing on the question of how humans discovered fire.

Field Notes: The group is miming a gathering of people all working outside. Some are sitting on the ground working, others are carrying things back and forth. They work silently. In this run through, as the children are pretending to be working together, they are trying harder to show that rain has started by exaggerating their gestures (shaking water off, shivering). They retreat into an implied shelter under the overhang. Derek turns and pretends to see lightning strike. He jumps up in fright and mimes shock. He goes toward the fire but then is repelled by the heat, stumbling backward. The other children don't see what he's doing: Their backs are to him. He gestures to them from the front of the cave, jumping up and down, grunting, running toward the cave opening and then back again in fright, but they are shivering and grunting among themselves, and they can't hear him. (I believe that these children truly can't hear him because they are so occupied in staying in character and hiding from the storm.) Finally he has to go in and touch their shoulders, pointing to the opening of the cave and gesturing for them to come with him. They wave him off and huddle closer together. As a last resort, he takes Gary by the arm and drags him out to the cave opening, show-ing him the fire and trying to reenact how it started. The other chil-dren follow him, and they watch in amazement, and amusement, as Derek reenacts the lightning strike. That, in itself, is quite a drama. Derek has stayed completely in character, as have the rest of the chil-dren. Not one word has been spoken.

The children who were watching and I were completely mesmerized by the whole scene, most especially as we observed Derek's frustration over his own inability to communicate what he had seen. As he performed, some of the children in the audience called out to him "Say something, say something!" and I understood how powerful this dramatic opportunity had been: There was no better way to realize what the achievement of language meant for humans. This was not the lesson I had hoped to see being constructed by the children, but it seemed a more powerful realiza-tion. Derek and his friends had actively constructed a possible story about the discovery of fire that had added meaning because of the comment he made through his movements about the importance of language, a com-ment he presented without words. The story, and his thinking behind it, was no less powerful for any of us because it was not voiced or written down.

This record represents the kind of surprise that I often have when working with the arts. What is extraordinary in all this is that, as a teacher, I am never disappointed by the results that the children achieve, and usually I am astonished to see the power and depth of their thinking process. Over the years of working with the arts, I have come to trust that if I am vigilant in my expectations for children, and consistent in reinforc-ing their efforts to make larger connections between ideas, the children will stretch for me.

EXTENDING AND ENRICHING THE CURRICULUM

For this particular class of children, the search for their past did not end with that experience. We continued casually to read different kinds of sources, as well as adding readings of creation myths. We talked about the discovery of metal and the beginnings of writing, war, and money. Our science talk questions expanded to include questions on the origin of languages and writing. We used the world map to trace the migration of humans northward from Africa, and we talked about how skin color related to migration and settlement patterns. Our respect for early humans expanded; as one child noted, "Those early humans must have been really smart, smarter than us even, because, like, they could do things we would never be able to do if we were there."

In February, after several children had expressed an interest in studying ancient Egypt, we began superficially to explore different aspects of that civilization. Then my student teacher, Karen Kleinkopf, and I realized, after observing several children's fascination with the process of mummification described in *Pyramid* (Macaulay, 1975), which they made us read over and over again, that these children were seriously interested in Egyptian rituals related to death. Karen began to work with several children on building a life-sized mummy from newspaper, muslin, and wheat paste. We decided that the most fruitful way to pursue the idea was to have the children reconstruct the parts of the funerary process that they could gather information on and that the only way to pursue this path was through an intensive use of the arts.

As work on the mummy progressed, we formed several study groups in the following categories: artists, a group of children who worked on mastering the style of Egyptian funerary paintings; artifacts, children who studied what was in the burial chamber; adornment, children who focused on clothing and jewelry; mummification, which included a study of the actual process of mummification; gods and goddesses; and burial rituals. The children spent two afternoons a week studying in their various groups, looking through books and resources, and drawing and sketching.

By March the mummy had been wrapped, and we divided into two larger study groups focusing on Egyptian funerary arts, including painting, decoration, and hieroglyphics, and Egyptian religion, focusing on the gods and the rituals of death. After a week of intense research, sketching, and talking, we began to expand our artwork. One group started a death mask for the mummy; others began to write hieroglyphic messages. A very nebulous but monumental idea was forming in all our minds that we would reconstruct a burial chamber. Clearly a study of this size posed a problem of both culmination and assessment. How could we bring all the children's work and thinking into a logical, aesthetic form? After we agreed as a class that we would try to build a burial chamber, the children took control, seeming to know how to proceed. Some children, armed with construction paper and tape, appropriated a classroom chair and table for furniture. Others began to bring in small collections of objects

Figure 8.1. Sketching life-sized figures on the chalk board.

for the mummy: necklaces, beads, rings, earrings, and statuettes, which they would tuck in the spaces between the mummy's layers of gauze.

The artists' group expressed concern that they needed to draw very large murals for the walls of the chamber. I put them to work sketching life-sized figures on the chalkboard. Each afternoon they would set the museum prints and books next to the chalkboard and stand on chairs to reach the top of the board, glancing at the books as they drew. They sketched and erased, sketched and erased (Figure 8.1). The work was slow and painstaking. Few children could figure out how to draw a life-sized figure free-hand. We had many frustrated discussions about how to draw a person from the profile, and, as I encouraged them to look at details—hands, feet, jewelry, and clothes—their figures improved. Finally they decided they were ready to transfer their chalk sketches onto mural paper.

Those children who had been studying burial rituals, after carefully scanning pictures in a story book, made a list of what we would need for the chamber: canopic chest and jars, baskets of food for the afterlife, games, weapons, and jewels. The canopic chest was built and decorated with pictures copied from museum books, and glass jars were covered with tissue paper and decorated with clay heads of the appropriate gods to represent the canopic jars (Figure 8.2). Four Japanese boys worked on the mummy's coffin, building it up with paper and cardboard, pasting on strips of paper to copy a design they had seen in a book (Figure 8.3). Two children made baskets to carry food into the burial chamber, and the artists began to paint the murals for the walls of the chamber.

The children who worked on the murals decided that they had to use hot colors and "old" colors for the walls. They used Craypas to do small details around the borders and paints for the larger figures. Those who had been studying hieroglyphics were commissioned to write the messages on the borders. As the murals were finished, I assembled all the artists and asked them to help one another look carefully at the work. I presented the idea that, in order to honor our mummy properly, we wanted the pictures to be as complete and excellent as possible, just as they would have

Figure 8.2. Decorating the canopic chest.

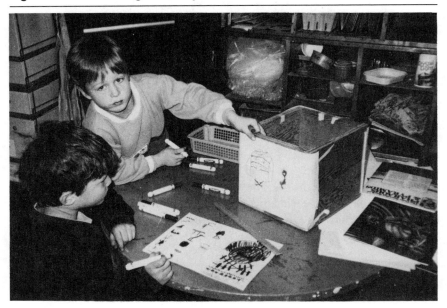

Figure 8.3. Working on the mummy's coffin.

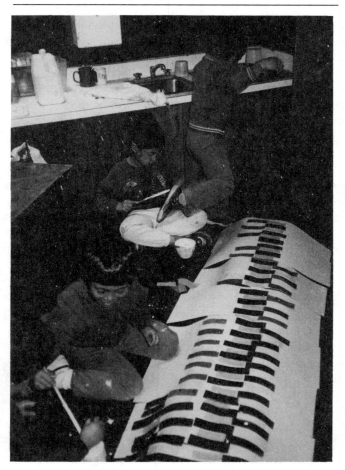

in ancient Egypt. In reality, my motive was the same. I wanted to be sure that each child saw the process of painting the mural as both an aesthetic and a critical exercise. What kinds of knowledge should the mural represent, and how could each child's representation be pushed to a higher level that reflected the kind of complex artistic problem solving they had been pursuing? I asked the children to help one another look carefully at the pictures. What parts did we like? What needed more work? What ideas were we trying to show through the murals?

We looked at Lila's mural first. Although Lila had done a good job, she had spent a lot of time saying she was finished well before the process was completed. Even as I encouraged her to do more, I knew that my words were old and she felt she had done enough, although, according to my standards, the picture was not quite finished. The children took my challenge very seriously, sitting as a group, scrutinizing Lila's painting. Donald commented that the dresses on Lila's mural needed to be colored more thoroughly to look good. He pointed out the spots where the white paper showed through. Other children encouraged Lila to finish the border, to go over the hieroglyphics so that they were clearer, to outline the figure's hair so it stood out from the black background and so the observer could see that the hair was a wig. Every single child, including Takayuki, who spoke little English, made critical comments, not in an unkind way, but in a critiquing tone. The children's seriousness reminded me of Elwyn Richardson's search with his students for positive ways to think about values in art; it also reminded me that that search was not necessarily an alienating process (Richardson, 1964).

In mid-April our mummy became Kamen, a pharaoh of ancient Egypt. We wrote Kamen's life story, and one child asked if we could have a real burial ritual. The class decided that that was a logical next step. Three boys who had studied the burial ceremonies acted as consultants and told us what roles the children could play, outlining other details we would have to arrange. According to their suggestion that we needed musical instruments for the procession, we began building instruments out of clay: bells, drums, shakers, and chimes. As the month closed, the children devised an "Opening of the Mouth" ritual and learned to walk in a procession. The two girls and two boys who had elected to play the priests involved in the ceremony improvised what they thought the priests might have said. They were very silly at first, but then they began to cue one another and developed the text of the ritual collaboratively.

In early May the children decided we were ready to enact the burial ritual. Our procession assembled in the hall with a long line of priests, officials, family members, servants, and official mourners. The children proceeded through the classrooms on the first floor: two children bearing the mummy, followed by canopic chest and jars, furniture, baskets of food, royal artifacts, and musical accompaniment (Figure 8.4). After making the circuit of the first-floor rooms and offices, they returned to an open area and arranged themselves in front of the mummy. Three children read the official version of Kamen's life:

THIS IS A HISTORY OF KAMEN'S LIFE

Kamen was born when his father, the Pharaoh Nunoko, was away in a war. Kamen lived for 96 years. When Kamen was thirteen, his fa-

Figure 8.4. The burial procession.

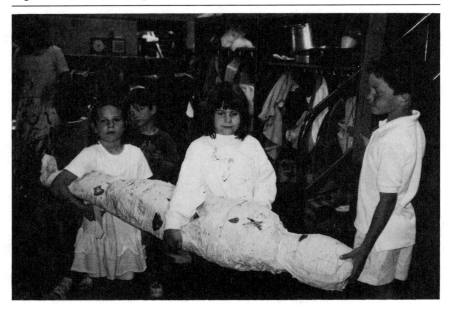

ther, who was blind, fell in a river, the Great Nile River, and drowned. Then Kamen became Pharaoh. Kamen had a very difficult life. There were many questions he couldn't answer, like, how long a person might live, and who would live forever. Once, when he was sixteen, the sun was so hot that the Nile River dried up little by little. The people couldn't get water and the hunting was bad. Their lambs died or became weak, and the plants died. The people had no food. When his people ran out of food, Kamen gave them food and water. He didn't eat better than them. He tried not to let people die. After a long sandstorm that covered half the country, he shared his homes with the Hooganis People (Hooganis is old Egyptian for homeless). Kamen was a good Pharaoh because he built many pyramids and won many wars. But he did not like wars. He liked people. Kamen had a wife, named Nana, and two children: a son named Unabaki, and a daughter named Chino. Pharaoh will be buried with his treasures and his power sword, Dee.

The priests performed the Opening of the Mouth, saying, as they touched the mummy's lips:

Open, Mouth, let the spirit out.
Spirit, rise up.
Open, eat, drink, and breathe.

Then Anubis, the god of tombs, turned toward the mourners and rang a bell. The official mourners took handfuls of flour (representing dust) and threw it on top of themselves. The other children took up the wailing, barely suppressing their mirth. Adults passing by gathered to watch the peculiar spectacle as flour drifted across the floor, bells and chimes rang, and mourners wailed. We were all almost beside ourselves with delight.

When the official mourners had run out of flour, Anubis asked everyone to rise, and we proceeded up the stairs into the burial chamber, placing Kamen in his sarcophagus with jewels and funerary objects. The children carefully arranged his furniture, put the portraits and other objects in their places, and Kamen was officially laid to rest (Figures 8.5 and 8.6).

Figure 8.5. Murals inside the burial chamber.

Figure 8.6. The burial chamber.

INCORPORATING THE ARTS ON ALL LEVELS

Thus ended a study that, had it been undertaken in traditional ways, would not have been as rich or long-lived in the minds of the children. Embedded in the final outcome were hours of thinking and study that enabled the children to place the content into a larger drama. That drama presented their story about death in ancient Egypt, and it could not have occurred without the incorporation of the arts on all the levels described in the beginning of this chapter: art as subject matter for study, art as a methodology for acquiring knowledge, and art as a way to build a story about that subject matter.

In the process of building this curriculum, these three aspects of artistic activity complemented and extended one another. As the children came to identify their interests and clarify their knowledge through deep involvement in the arts, they also explored the techniques and aesthetics of other cultures, both as artists and as would-be archaeologists and art historians. At the same time, the processes of drawing, painting, movement, and writing helped them build the context and layers of their stories. By engaging the children's abilities to reconstruct thinking in distinctly metaphoric ways, ways that synthesize and expand understanding, we opened the curriculum for all of us to learn and grow.

Yet this process of developing curricula with children opens up another conundrum for teachers. As a teacher-researcher, when I begin to keep track of the meanings children bring to school, I often find that what they want to know as a class differs from what the adults in schools want them to know. I am not always convinced that adult agendas are any more valid than children's agendas, and as I scrutinize children's drawings, conversations, writings, and play for meanings, I am compelled to follow their interests more readily than those of the adults who write curriculum guides but never know the children.

Studies of early humans and ancient Egypt by first and second graders are rarely included in the social studies curricula of most schools. Effective teachers who keep track of their students' expressive, emotive, and intellectual interests cannot develop responsive curricula from a platter of neatly bound notebooks. They hunt, gather, are clairvoyant about the future, reenvision the past, scrutinize the present, and consider the broad context of the world their students encounter every day. They attempt to construct a classroom environment and a curriculum that offer a transcendent view of knowledge: knowledge that reflects the immediacy and passion of children's curiosity, that includes the structures that build literacy in all disciplines, and that is grounded in a wide range of expressive opportunities.

9

Arts as Epistemology

Enabling Children to Know What They Know

> *Or if you don't know what a wing is, and how it is made, you can draw it, and then you know.*
>
> Juan, age 6

One afternoon in early June, six children and I crowd around a butterfly box watching a painted lady chrysalis twitch and turn as the butterfly inside struggles to break free. Juan, who is seated on a chair next to the box, holds a clipboard on his lap and is carefully sketching the scene. This is his third sketch of the day chronicling the final stage in the life cycle of the butterfly (Figure 9.1). It will complete a collection he began in early May, when mealworms arrived in our first-grade classroom. As he draws, the children agonize over the butterfly's plight. They have been watching since early that morning, and they all wonder if the butterfly will ever get out. Sophia smiles to herself and then begins to hum a tune.

"I'll sing it out," she says.

"Yeah, let's sing it out!" agrees Matthew, and all the children begin to improvise a song. Juan looks up, smiles, and continues to sketch.

Events such as these have become almost commonplace in my classroom. Over the course of the school year, this particular class of children questioned, researched, wondered, and discussed their way through a wide variety of subject matter and concepts. What distinguished their learning process from that of many other children, however, was the presence of the arts as an integral part of their curriculum: as a methodology for acquiring knowledge, as subject matter, and as an array of expressive opportunities. Drawing and painting, music, movement, dramatic enactment, poetry, and storytelling: Each domain, separately and together, became part of their total repertoire as learners.

By describing the development of a unit on insects, this chapter specifically relates how the arts can play an essential role in forming and extend-

Figure 9.1. Juan's sketch of the emerging butterfly.

ing all aspects of a particular topic of study. While Chapter 8 provides a general survey of the place of the arts in eliciting children's stories about learning, this chapter is more focused on how I, as a teacher, use the arts to respond to the developmental needs of my students within the context of a required science curriculum.

A UNIT ON LIFE CYCLES

The concept of life cycles, which informed our study throughout, was the focus of several months of work for my first-grade class. Eighteen children, from a range of socioeconomic, racial, and cultural backgrounds, and including four different language groups, participated in this study from late winter through the month of June. What happened in this class could happen in any class of children. Each group brings a wide range of life experience to school, and, though we are often initially separated by language, cultural, and racial barriers, I have learned that the creative arts, rather than labeling our differences, enable us to celebrate them.

Juan arrived in September from Venezuela, speaking no English but filled with joy at being in school. As I struggled during our first few weeks together to find out what he could and could not do (and found out that, according to my teacher's agenda, he could not do many things), Juan very graciously attempted to help me understand what he could do. He would tolerate a few minutes of my informal assessment activities and then use his one word of English: "Paint?" he would suggest cheerfully, and by that time I would agree. Paint, for Juan, meant drawing, painting, modeling, or constructing, and it was his passion. As the weeks passed, I continued to be amazed by his talent and frustrated by his inability to learn the alphabet and basic reading-readiness skills. However, Juan's own nonchalance about the process of learning to read and write was some-what contagious, and I began to see that his art was presenting what he had already learned at home and in school as well as what he desired to learn. It soon became clear that our forays into the world of number and letter recognition would be fruitless without Juan's skill as an artist. His visual representations became a catalogue of science information and sci-ence questions, and that information began to provide material for his involvement in reading and writing and learning a new language. As Juan drew, we built a reading and speaking vocabulary from his pictures, and that vocabulary, together with his interest in representing science, also became the subject matter of his writing.

Juan was teaching me once again a lesson that I seem to have to relearn each year: When given the opportunity, listen to the children. They will show you what they know and how they learn best, and often that way is not the teacher's way. Because I am a teacher, my unspoken agenda is shaped by academic expectations: I am supposed to present concepts and skills, and the children are supposed to master those skills and concepts. Unfortunately, the journey toward mastery of a subject is often inextricably tied to instruments of assessment, presentation, and communication that are designed by and for teachers. Tests, workbook pages, teacher-led discussions, textbooks, charts — each of these assumes a commonality of experience that the children in a classroom may not have. Each artificially separates the process of mastery from that of individual expression. Each of these excludes the full participation of some portion of the population I teach.

Developing a multi-arts curriculum allows me to follow the children's own expressive interests while also using the artistic process as an integral part of the identification and expansion of their knowledge in different areas. This method goes beyond the use of art as an enhancement or enrichment of an already established curriculum and places the arts as central to the completion of the curricular process. For both teacher and child, the arts offer an expanded notion of classroom discourse that is not solely grounded in linear, objective language and thinking but rather recognizes the full range of human potential for expression and understanding.

From the first days of our study of the life cycle of insects, we used basic creative and critical thinking skills to identify our existing knowledge base. What did these children know about insects, and what did they want to know? As a group, we brainstormed, sharing our common knowledge, and in the process generated questions we wanted to answer. Later we drew a semantic map to extend and relate our ideas.

WHAT WE KNOW ABOUT INSECTS	QUESTIONS ABOUT INSECTS
Birds eat them.	Are caterpillars insects?
They have six legs.	How many legs do beetles have?
Some are furry or slimy.	Do all insects have legs?
Some help trees.	Do all insects fly?
Some fly.	How do fireflies light up?
Some eat fruit.	Why do fireflies light up?
Some people eat them.	How do insects grow?
They could destroy the earth.	How do insects swallow?
Some eat wood.	Do they have teeth?
Some live underground.	How old can an insect get?
Some are dangerous.	How do they smell?
Some insects eat other insects.	How many kinds are there?
Most have antennae.	Do insects have lips?
Some have wings and don't fly.	Do they all hop?
Some insects are poisonous.	Do they smell with antennae?
Some help plants.	
Some insects eat plants.	
Some insects have stingers.	

Our study then began in earnest with observations of mealworms. We observed, sketched, and took notes on their behavior. Juan discovered in our second day of sketching that one of his mealworms was in the process of shedding its skin. Thus began the first in his series of meticulous sketches, both from live animals and from nonfiction books about insects. As a class, we spent the afternoons in the first week sketching, studying books and photographs, discussing entomological drawings by different artists, and observing the mealworms and caterpillars. On Friday we showed some of the sketches and talked about what we were learning. The children were very impressed by the work, and those who had not been sketching asked Juan how he got so good. "I practice a lot," he said, and our discussion continued about why we were sketching.

DAVID: I'd heard people talk about this thing. I think it was a praying mantis, but I didn't know what it was. So I looked at a book, and then I drew it, and then I knew what it was (Figure 9.2).

JUAN: Or if you don't know what a wing is and how it's made you can draw it and then you know.

A few days later, Adam was seated by himself, trying to sketch a picture of a monarch butterfly from a book. Since September Adam had struggled with fine-motor tasks, such as drawing, cutting, or construction, but he was so impressed with the work of other children that he had decided to try to do a sketch. As I watched, he was quite absorbed and had finished one wing, but the second wing was more difficult. He threw down his pencil, and I could see he was going to cry.

"Don't stop, Adam," I said, and he nodded, wiped his eyes, and picked up the pencil.

Juan walked over to see what was wrong and offered a few suggestions. "You don't have to make it perfect today. Just draw it, then do

Figure 9.2.   David's sketch of a praying mantis.

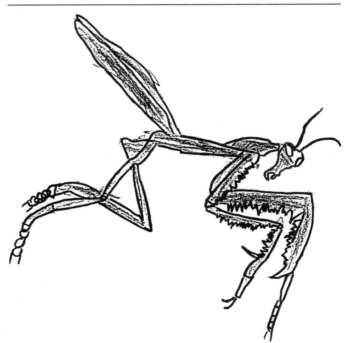

Figure 9.3. Adam's drawing of a monarch butterfly.

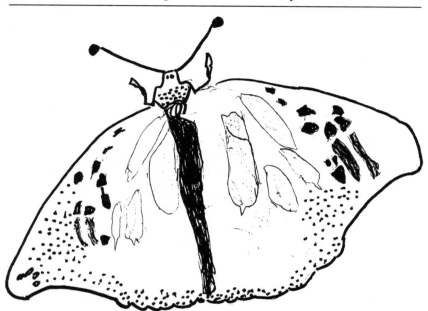

more tomorrow." Adam went back to work. A few minutes later I saw him using the length of his forefinger to gauge how big the wingspread in the picture was. Juan came over to check but said nothing. Adam continued until it was time to go home, working on the picture for another week until it was finished. He had done a beautiful, meticulous job, and he asked if I could make copies for the class to share (Figure 9.3).

It is intense artistic activity like this that begins in the early stages of learning and continues throughout a study that enables children to become immersed in a subject. The deep involvement in representing the form of an insect, whether it is one that has been observed or one only pictured in books, expands the child's basic knowledge of that organism and his or her ability to represent it in both thought and form. For Juan, visual representation was a natural process. It was his method for examining his world, as well as his means of externalizing what he was learning for others to share. For Adam, who excelled in reading, writing, and abstract thought, but who often had a difficult time communicating and interacting with other children, the artistic process of drawing the monarch butterfly expanded his own boundaries of symbolic representation and gave him a new way to reach out to other children. Adam often approached the learning process in a highly verbal and discursive manner, delighting in puns and playing on words or ideas in his speech and writing. These abstractions sometimes eluded his classmates, and thus the act of presenting himself in a visually compelling form became a new challenge for him as a learner.

INCLUDING THE POETIC VOICE

One day early in our study, Carolyn made a special request. She had finished reading most of our nonfiction resource books, but she wanted to know if I had any poems about insects. I was sure I did, but I wondered why. She explained:

> A poem is a little short, and it tells you some things in a funny way. But a science book, it tells you things like on the news . . . But in a poem, it's more . . . the poem teaches you, but not just with words.

Carolyn, whom I would often find throughout the year alone in the coat-cubbies writing poetry on scraps of paper, had reminded me that I had constructed my plans and gathered my resources too narrowly. Throughout the year as a class, we had used poetry as a way to gain more insight into whatever subject we were studying. Carolyn began to collect poems to read to the class about insects, and I reconsidered the place of poetry in this study. Her interest in metaphoric ways of knowing is not an isolated one. Poetry sometimes provides children with a window of insight that is broader than that offered in even the best nonfiction resources. Poetic form is often more suited to the thinking and writing of children than prose; it is spare, yet rich with sense impressions. It is a medium in which the images of wonder, curiosity, and analogic thinking, which so often characterize children's language, can flourish.

In the next week, our observations of insects continued outside, where each child found an insect habitat, observed the insect, sketched the habitat, and wrote field notes. Upon returning one afternoon, we shared our findings and began to discuss the relationships between our classroom study and our outdoor explorations. Soon after, we read *The Inch Boy* (Morimoto, 1986), a Japanese folk tale that describes the experiences of a character who never grows larger than an inch tall. The children were fascinated by the notion of living in the world as a tiny being. Adam wondered out loud what the world might be like for a tiny velvet spider mite: He had made the connection that I hoped would occur.

Jeffrey offered, "Well, what you might think is a hill would probably only be a pebble or a big piece of dirt."

"And," added Carolyn, "you might never see the blue sky, only just green and green and you'd think the top of the world was green." These ideas produced a lot of commotion, and before we left the meeting I asked the children to write a poem in the persona of an insect that they had observed. Sean chose the ant:

Ant
by Sean

I pretend I'm a ant
running and dodging birds.
Grass feels tickly under my feet.
Big trees shade me.
I climb a bush and I see buildings
houses and even other bugs too.
And then I see a watermelon seed
and I go off to carry it away with my friends.

MOVING TOWARD DEEPER UNDERSTANDINGS

After two weeks, the mealworms and caterpillars were pupating, and these observations, together with our classroom research and outdoor experiences, offered an opportunity for us to compare the life cycles of several insects. Many children had gained a great deal of new knowledge about different insects and their habits, and their understanding had been shared in a variety of ways. I encouraged the children to relate and expand their knowledge through movement and dramatization. In small groups, they presented either the life cycle of an animal they had observed or one they had researched. Each group conferred, agreeing on an insect to present, and then after some rehearsal mimed the stages of that insect's life cycle. Sometimes each member of a small group enacted a different stage in that cycle, while in other groups the members played out the transformation in unison. Brian and Roberto lay on the floor, legs tucked against their sides, mirroring the slightly visible legs on the mealworm pupa. I was surprised when they portrayed the transition from mealworm to pupa with such accuracy that even the timing of the twitching of the pupa was realistic.

For Brian, who might easily be labeled as having an attention deficit because of his constant motion and distractibility, the action and focus of the movement experience demonstrated how carefully he had observed and examined the mealworms, and it also showed that Brian had the ability to translate his ideas into a kinetic modality with great clarity. By offering him access to the arts of movement and enactment, I have been able to see Brian's strengths: how carefully he observes and analyzes every detail of the world around him, and how creatively he solves challenging problems. Those strengths are often obscured by his behavioral problems, but when Brian works through movement and drama, the behaviors that handicap him in another situation become his gifts.

One of the more difficult tasks that I face as a teacher is moving children like Brian beyond the level of acquiring new knowledge and ideas and asking them to synthesize and apply their ideas to new and different contexts. It would be easy for me to take a very basic approach to assessment and simply ask children to regurgitate what they have learned, and we would have reached our goals: Tell me the facts of the life cycle of insects and label the stages on this diagram. Yet the act of moving beyond simple knowledge acquisition toward true assimilation of learning is the challenge for most children, and the process of assessing their learning in a way that stimulates that growth is my challenge. True knowing means transformation and change, and it is that level of learning that I hope for but often find difficult to offer as a possibility to the children.

Fortunately, however, when given the opportunity, the children will provide me with ideas to accomplish this goal. Sean, who is a talented artist, had become fascinated by the notion of relative size. He asked if he and Jeffrey could do a picture to go with his poem. They spent a week working on a huge mural, drawing towering blades of grass, large rocks, and giant sunflowers, then adding tiny insects trudging up the huge plants (Figure 9.4). Sean's fascination, like Carolyn's, expanded my ideas of what was possible both for these children to grasp conceptually and for all of us to achieve aesthetically. The union of critical and creative thinking that I had repeatedly observed taking place in the production of the mural, in Sophia's song about the struggle to complete a cycle, in Brian's translation of biological change into movement—this interaction that constantly occurs in the process of artistic activity is the key to an expansive curriculum.

DIVERSIFYING THE ART EXPERIENCE

Like the children, I must remain open to the potential of the arts to expand both my knowledge of the children I teach and my creative insight into the ongoing development of a curriculum. Many times I seem to miss opportunities to expand the children's experience because I am unable to see beyond the boundaries of my own goals for their learning. For exam-

Figure 9.4. Detail from Sean and Jeffrey's mural.

ple, Juan, our keen observer, in his careful scrutiny of all the pictures in our resource books, discovered a picture of a cocoon we had had in our room for several months but were unable to identify. The description in the book confirmed what we had observed in early May, when hundreds of tiny caterpillars came streaming out of the cocoon and then promptly took up residence in our garbage garden. (A garbage garden is one in which children bring in things from home, which we then plant in planters to see what will grow. There is no limit on what can be planted. In the past, we have tried to grow, with varying degrees of success: rubber bands, ginger, garlic, toy cars, marbles, paper clips, potato skins, and egg shells.) There, the caterpillars crawled through the planters and wrapped themselves in pieces of leaves and potato skins. We were astonished and puzzled. The little caterpillars were, we read, called bagworms. Alison, who had brought us the cocoon in late winter, was terribly excited about the discovery. For several weeks we watched the survivors grow amidst the potato plants, which they preferred. They continued to cover themselves in leaves and debris.

At the same time, eight children, including Alison, had become involved in reading and sharing different why-and-how stories, such as *Why Mosquitoes Buzz in People's Ears* (Aardema, 1975) and selections from the *Just So Stories* (Kipling, 1902/1978). For me, Juan's discovery of the bagworm and its habits, which struck us all as ludicrous but wonderful, as well as the children's interest in stories that offered humorous explanations of animal adaptation, seemed to mesh with our class discussions of how animals and humans adapt to survive in their environments.

My realization that these events coalesced also addressed the challenge of developing an integrated arts curriculum that provides a range of arts experiences that will offer opportunities for *all* children to communicate their new knowledge and expanded understanding of the world. Every child is not a visual artist, like Juan or Sean, though some are; every child does not find expanded meaning through the poetic voice, like Carolyn, though many do; and every child cannot represent an idea in movement or sound, like Brian and Roberto. The challenge, then, is to ensure that the range of experiences is broad enough to reveal each child's voice and that those experiences spring from events that all the children have shared in common.

Alison, whose shy demeanor and sparse language give an impression of austere silence, is, in fact, a storyteller. Storytellers are often unknowingly discovered in the daily classroom event of sharing time, as Jiana's story has shown us. However, because talk and telling in many classrooms is generally dominated by the teacher, the talent of many storytellers remains concealed. Yet storytelling, as we know from studies of culture and folklore, is a way to pass on knowledge and information and is also a dramatic event. Like drawing, music, and movement, it is also a preferred medium through which some children more adeptly clarify their relationship to the world and to their companions.

When I placed the challenge before the children of taking their new knowledge about insect life cycles and applying it to a different problem, Alison decided, with a few other children, that she wanted to make up a story to tell the class. Her story would explain how the bagworm came to carry the bag. At the same time, several other children decided to invent completely new insects based on their generalized knowledge of insects and draw or construct their imaginary habitat and life cycle. Alison proceeded to write a 12-page story about the bagworm, which she edited and revised, realizing at one point that she had forgotten to explain allegorically that the female bagworm never comes out of the bag. When she finished, she told us a story in which the bagworm went from a tiny, unnoticed nuisance to a huge creature that ate everything in sight. In order to save themselves from the wrath of humans, the female worms decided to construct a bag to hide in, and they invited the males to join them. "But," said Alison in conclusion, "the males only stayed in the bags until they turned into moths, but the females were too scared to ever come all the way out, so they even laid their eggs inside of the bag, and then they died there." What Alison had described was the correct life cycle of those strange animals, but her vehicle for presenting it was entirely of her own invention. The story enabled her to transform her observations and study of insects, as well as her involvement with a new literary genre, into a unique language event. In effect, Alison was creating her own folklore about a phenomenon she had observed in the world.

WORKING WITH MISCONCEPTIONS

As Alison finished her project, other children created insects that were adapted to completely unique circumstances. I observed Ronit drawing a picture of her insect, the buttercup beauty bug. She had labeled it with two parts: head and body. I saw this and asked her to rethink what body parts an insect had. She looked at her drawing and back at me, then got up and went to fetch her science journal, opening it up to refer to a diagram we had used a few weeks earlier when we observed the mealworm beetles. On a new piece of paper, Ronit correctly redesigned her insect to include three body parts, colored it in with a bright yellow crayon, and began a third drawing of the insect in its habitat. As she drew, she told me it was going to live in the grass when it was an adult, and that it would get its food from buttercups.

"This is the actual size of my insect," she said as she drew a line that was about two inches long. Then she stopped, her eyes widened, and she gulped.

"Oops, that's way too big," and she grabbed the eraser once again. After drawing a line that was much smaller, she continued, "Aren't I smart? 'Cause I was thinking of him in the buttercups, so I had to make him smaller, or someone would come along and be terrified" (Figure 9.5). For Ronit, the art experience at this time became an opportunity to find out what she did or did not understand and to rethink her ideas in a new form. Watching her work on an artistic problem, I was able to see that

Figure 9.5. Ronit's *Buttercup Beauty Bug.*

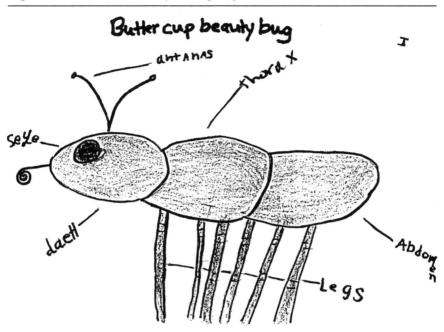

Ronit had not understood some basic information, but I could also observe her quickly correcting herself and thinking through the problems that are inherent in this type of activity.

Looking back over Ronit's work from the beginning of the unit, I found other points at which her artwork had revealed basic misconceptions. In the early days of sketching and defining what was an insect and what was not, Ronit had sifted through the large pile of photographs and prints I had assembled of insects, bugs, and spiders, selecting a spider's web as her focus (Figure 9.6). She spent a great deal of time composing the picture, and the result was quite effective aesthetically, but when I asked her to explain why she chose the web, she pointed out that it was a home for an insect. Her explanation, which reflects a common misconception, did not depreciate the value of the picture for us, but let me know that I had to return with her to a closer inspection of the prints.

Later in our studies, when the children were observing insects outside and taking field notes, Ronit wrote the following poem:

> Insects crawl
> and some make cocoons.

Others make just a plain living
with what they are.

I found this piece of writing charming, as I had her picture of the spider's web, but I pointed out to Ronit that the poem did not describe what she had just observed outside, when she was following several ants around. She agreed, and a few days later I sent her outside again with clipboard and pencil to try the assignment once more. This time, she watched and sketched, and wrote more carefully, describing what she had actually seen, rather than playing with language and overgeneralized knowledge.

Figure 9.6. Ronit's sketch of a spider's web.

I saw a ant hole in some grass and I lost my ant
but I tried to catch flies with Fuyuka and Yuri.
But they were too fast.
They were hiding in the sun. They were green flies.

An extremely creative child, Ronit, in her love of drawing, writing, and language, showed great flexibility of thinking and sensitivity to imagery, but those traits interfered with her ability to amass correct information about the insects she was studying. For her the range of art experiences were directed at developing observation skills that would enable her to distinguish between what she was seeing and the stories she imagined. Those activities stimulated her to clarify her basic information while also engaging her aesthetic viewpoint. By the end of our study Ronit had written a story about a caterpillar that showed how basic observation and attendance to correct information had meshed with her fertile imagination.

WHY DO CATERPILLARS MAKE A COCOON?
by Ronit

Once upon a time a baby caterpillar was born. He was actually the cutest caterpillar you ever saw. He was green and had teeny little feelers. His eyes were sparkling like glitter. But later on in his future his brothers and sisters were complaining to him. "You're too young to do this. You're too young to do that!" He was really having a hard life. Then finally he had enough. So he snuck away from home and wandered off into the forest. But on the way a hungry bird swooped down and flew with him in his beak. But when the bird saw a worm crawling up his nest he dropped the little caterpillar and went straight for the other one. The little caterpillar was safe but he had some little pains in his back. The little caterpillar went on crawling. He would have been fine if a little boy had not found him under some rocks and he took him home and put the little caterpillar in a jelly jar. But then the little boy brang the jelly jar outside. But by mistake the boy left the jelly jar opened and the little caterpillar was safe. So the little caterpillar went on crawling and crawling. He'd had a long day. Night fell. The little caterpillar went to sleep. The next day the little caterpillar woke up quite early. He decided what he wanted to do most of all was make a cocoon so he could get some peace and quiet and he set to work. He spinned a cocoon with silk thread. Soon enough he was no longer a caterpillar. He was a co-

coon. Days passed and the little caterpillar stayed there and one day
the cocoon began to rumble and he was a butterfly at last.

USING THE ARTS FOR TRANSFORMATION AND CHANGE

Late in June, as we approached the end of school, we talked about
our studies of life cycles. I asked the children to brainstorm with me about
what they thought of when they heard the word *metamorphosis*. Here is
what they said:

Metamorphosis

egg	— mealworm	— pupa	— beetle		
egg	— tadpole	— frog			
egg	— caterpillar	— chrysalis	— butterfly		
egg	— caterpillar	— cocoon	— moth		
egg	— larvae	— mosquito			
seed	— plant	— flower	— fruit		
water	— rain	— snow	— ice		
wind	— tornado	— cyclone	— waterspout		
egg	— dinosaur	— reptile	— bird		
egg	— baby	— grownup	— death	— dirt	

We gathered for a movement and drama session after this, and I asked
the children to describe, through movement, a metamorphosis that they
had thought about or seen. Most of the children presented impressions of
one of the ideas listed above. Finally, Brian, Jeffrey, and Lea, who had
asked to go last, took their turn. They began with Brian enclosed between
Lea's and Jeffrey's arms, as if in an embrace. Slowly, Lea and Jeffrey
opened their arms and lifted Brian above them with his arms outstretched.
He stood there as long as they could hold him and then the three toppled
over together, flattened against the ground. Brian leapt up, took out an
imaginary pencil, and began to write on Jeffrey's stomach. The other
children, who had been mystified, jumped to their feet and shouted.
"Tree! It's the life cycle of a tree!"

What we all understood by the end of this study was more than a
collection of ideas about life cycles. What we understood from our experiences with the arts as subject matter and as inspiration was that knowing
was not just telling something back as we had received it. Knowing meant
transformation and change as well as a gradual awareness of what we
had learned. For both children and teacher, the arts offer opportunities
for reflection on the content and the process of learning, and they foster a

deeper level of communication about what knowledge is and who is truly in control of the learning process. As a pedagogical standard, the integration of the arts offers a rich resource for educators to infuse the learning experience at all levels with expansive and challenging perspectives.

The arts make it possible for all children, regardless of their differences, to participate fully in the process of education. They transcend the limitations placed on those children, such as Juan and Brian, whose language, culture, or life experience is outside the mainstream of American schooling. They challenge children such as Adam to expand their boundaries of personal expression and communication. They confirm the perspectives of children like Alison, Sean, and Carolyn, whose modes of communication and expression do not fit the predominant classroom discourse. They enable all children to recognize the breadth and depth of their learning.

Conclusion

A Noiseless Patient Spider

A noiseless patient spider,
I mark'd where on a little promontory it stood isolated,
Mark'd how to explore the vacant vast surrounding,
It launch'd forth filament, filament, filament out of itself,
Ever unreeling them, ever tirelessly speeding them.

And you O my soul where you stand,
Surrounded, detached, in measureless oceans of space,
Ceaselessly musing, venturing, throwing, seeking the
    spheres to connect them,
Till the bridge you will need be formed, till the
    ductile anchor hold,
Till the gossamer thread you fling catch somewhere,
O my soul.

                                    Walt Whitman, 1868

When speaking about my work to students, teachers, and parents, I have often used this poem to frame my thoughts. It speaks both to the work that I see children doing in their lives in and outside of school and to the kinds of explorations that I participate in as a parent, teacher, and teacher-researcher. For some reason, I am not able to separate the children's and my search for knowledge and greater understanding in the microcosmic setting of the classroom from what I perceive to be a larger and less easily described search for meaning in the world. Whitman's metaphors of spider, and then soul, capture the intimate nature of what can happen in the classroom. We are in the business of locating ourselves into the larger framework of being.

Once again, I descend into the domain of the aboriginal, equating reading with magic and classroom life with a search for an understanding of soul. It is a messy undertaking, but one that the stories in this book address. There are many more stories that I am still pondering that address it as well. There are the questions that children begin to ask in our second year of association that are openings for more personal conversations: questions that have to do with my life and my past, with the nature and structure of my family, with how we are the same and how we are different, with my thinking about the children's own hard questions.

There are the stories children write in writing time over periods of weeks. These stories are filled with unspoken questions about what it means to be compassionate and authentic in one's life. They are filled with glimpses of transformative language, and they reflect the "musing, venturing, throwing, seeking the spheres to connect them." I believe that my stories about the children in this book also reflect the filaments we throw out to form the "bridge" Whitman speaks about.

Thus I find it difficult to write the conclusion of this book in any voice other than that of the teacher who is engaged in this collaborative search for meaning. By the very nature of my philosophical stance as a teacher-researcher, I cannot generalize about the work I have described to other settings, nor can I describe broad new methodological structures. Rather, I can only speak about my current understanding of children's thinking and how I conceptualize the vast domain that the term *language* embraces. These understandings take form in habitual practices that have a daily impact on how I teach and in the kind of learning environment I work to build with my students.

Because these ideas have evolved as a result of my work as a teacher-researcher using ethnographic methods, I believe they reflect more an ontological and philosophical approach to the act of teaching than strictly methodological or paradigmatic outcomes. That is, once one looks imaginally at the classroom, one has *only* the ability to look imaginally. The nature of imagination is that it never perceives the world in the same way twice, yet in the process of reimagining the world, that world is forever altered. I would maintain that that attitude reflects the true nature of teaching and the classroom at its best.

In this last chapter, then, I hope to accomplish two things: first to speak about those aspects of classroom language that centrally affect my practice; and second, to describe how the movement from teacher to teacher-researcher forever changes the nature of the teacher's work. I believe that, as in the rest of this book, the second concept will be embedded in the stories that describe the first.

RETHINKING THE LANGUAGES OF LEARNING

This book has focused on a broad definition of narrative as a way to gain more insight into children's thinking and as a way to reimagine teaching and learning. As such, classroom language is very broadly defined and embraces many different domains. Within the context of this broad definition, there are four aspects of language in the classroom that I must explicitly pay attention to if I am best to serve the children I teach. These aspects represent an overarching approach to classroom language that applies to both myself and the children, and they permeate all aspects of our communication on a daily basis. In summative terms, they include the following behaviors:

Valuing silence
Using language self-consciously
Contextualizing language
Exploring multiple texts

Each of these is represented in the content of this book and in the tone in which it is written, and the last stories I would like to tell relate examples of the larger pictures from which these understandings have emerged.

Valuing Silence

"I know why the leaves turn different colors," Vera, a 6-year-old, said in a science talk that took place in my classroom. "They're really that color . . . but you see the chlorine, whatever I mean . . . in the winter it stops coming up. You could even say that they're . . . dressing up in chlorine, and it's Halloween, that if you take off your coat, you get back to what you really are."

This is a story about taking off your coat and getting back to what you really are.

Teaching can be a wonderfully absorbing profession. It enables one to be completely taken in by the world of children and their learning. It is, for some people like myself, a consuming endeavor in which I can expend hours planning for and thinking about a class full of children. In September of 1989, the first week of that school year, as I was quickly sinking into my pattern of complete immersion in the life of the classroom, I accidentally came across a letter that had just been posted on the bulletin board in the teachers' room. I had stopped to read the walls in an effort to grasp one last thread of outside communication. The letter was dated in June, and though it was September, I read it anyway. It looked important. It was clearly a letter from a grown-up. The letter, which was from Sarah Michaels of the Literacies Institute at the Education Development Center in Newton, Massachusetts, invited teachers who might be interested in learning more about teacher research and the language of the classroom to join the Brookline Teacher Researcher Seminar. It described a weekly seminar in which teachers looked together at children's talk and at the same time learned about doing research in the classroom, and it asked interested teachers to attend a colloquium in August. Clearly, I had missed that deadline. But I was intrigued and contacted Sarah. The following week I received a call from Ann Phillips, who was the seminar leader at that time, and she encouraged me to join the group.

I began going to the seminar the following week, and right away I noticed two things. One was that this was a seminar that was clearly for teachers, and although researchers were present, they were co-partic- ipants and did not lead the group, acting rather as consultants and col- leagues. The second was that the pace of the seminar seemed very, very slow. There were a lot of silences. Talk was slowed down and wait-time was protracted. I was used to a fast pace, both in my teaching and in my talking, and I wondered if the pace was slow and there were a lot of silences because no one had anything to say. Still, I was terribly interested in the readings and discussions about talk, and I started to think carefully about their implications for my teaching. I later realized that everyone in the group had many things to say and that the silence was the result of careful use of language. Gradually, this kind of silence moved into my work in the classroom.

It is important for me to point out that the school year of 1989–90 was also the year that I was visited by what I now affectionately call the class from hell. The class from hell was not my first such class; every teacher of longevity has had several of these. They can arrive unexpectedly in any random September, but usually at a time when you are beginning to feel that you have finally gotten the practice of teaching in hand. Predicting their arrival is not easy, however, because the creation of such a class requires a subtle mixing of different personalities and social interac- tions that no one can really foresee. This particular class included 20 creative, independent, and active first graders with a few very significant problems. It is intriguing that they were the first class that I approached formally as a teacher-researcher. I say *formally* because I had always been involved in informal thinking and writing about my classroom practice, but this was my first experience in looking systematically and intensely at practice from the standpoint of a particular research discipline, that of sociolinguistics and ethnography, and this was the first time I had named what I did as teacher research. So this class was the first class that I approached from this new vantage point.

In September, as I realized the magnitude of the teaching task before me, I also began to understand in what ways an orientation to children's talk and the different discourses they bring to school would enable me to focus on each child's stories rather than their collective behaviors. I became very involved in researching what I now call science talks. Although I had originally started these talks as a way to begin to answer my own questions about how young children talk about science, I found that my work with the seminar and with the science talks enabled both me and the children to carry on a continuous dialogue about science and what it was. That was an immensely positive focus for this class and me, as we struggled daily to live and work together. As I worked intensely with audiotaping and painstakingly transcribing our science talks, I also became very engaged in the literature on classroom discourse, and quite subtly (it was imperceptible at first) I started to think about silence, most particularly my silence — or lack of it. I began to feel uncomfortable with the presence of my voice in the science talks, and eventually in late November I made the decision, which I have described earlier in this book, to be quiet.

And I was quiet in science talks for the next six months. It was torture. (Remember, this is the class from hell, and not only did they move a lot, they also fought and made a great deal of noise.) As soon as I was quiet, though, the children without hesitation took control of the process and the content of the science talks. Sometimes in the midst of these talks, I felt that I was descending into a great abyss and would never, never crawl out again. Their words milled around me; everywhere I looked there seemed to be disorder. I could not make sense of their ideas, could not follow the trails of their thoughts. Only when I began to look at the transcripts with other members of the seminar, and as we considered the data together, did I realize that there was a great deal of coherence and depth to the children's thinking. I also realized that what was afflicting me most was that their talk and their thinking did not proceed in the same directions, and with the same style, as mine; that I could not effectively control the discourse because their discourse was so different from the one I had become accustomed to using; and finally, that I was no longer sure whose style of talking about science was more appropriate: their's or mine.

What, you might be wondering, has all this to do with getting back to what you really are? I now realize that, from the beginning of my participation in the seminar as a teacher-researcher, I have been walking back toward understanding my early relationship to language and how it has shaped my work as a student, a teacher, and a researcher. This journey began with my discomfort with the pace and silences of the seminar, continued throughout my struggle to be quiet in my classroom, and has lengthened as seminar members read, write, and talk together about the place of language in their lives. It eventually led to my realization that children's stories move beyond spoken and written language and are embodied in their songs, dances, and pictures—and that those stories also begin with silence.

I believe that this journey will extend indefinitely as seminar members consider together over and over again what the notion of teacher research means within the context of our group, as we struggle to find out how to talk about this field and the new structures and relationships it requires with our students, our colleagues, our school systems, and the larger research community. The close examination of our thinking, which the seminar allows and provides a time and place for, enables us to see the process of teaching and research as a story that is never finished, a story whose ending is unknown, a story that, as Ann Phillips often says, "we haven't yet developed the language to talk about."

And now, although my journey has just begun, I am finally comfortable with the spaces between the words. I see how creating a small space for both reflecting upon and inspecting the boundaries of classroom discourse can allow both children and teachers to move beyond what is given to what is possible. I have come to believe that it is important for teachers, as Grumet says, to "harvest silence . . . to construct a special place for ourselves if our work . . . is to achieve the clarity, communication and insight of aesthetic practice—if it is, in short, to be research and not merely representation" (Grumet, 1988, pp. 88–89).

Using Language Self-Consciously

In this book I have described the kinds of classroom events that I, as a teacher-researcher, closely document. It is clear that my choices in this case relate to my own interests and history as a teacher and a learner. I believe those things are inseparable. It is also clear that, as I more carefully examine my actions and perceptions as a teacher, the act of teaching becomes more self-conscious. I begin to notice things that I had not intended to see but that are no less important for my practice. Thus the boundaries between teaching and research blur: What we perceive in either role changes the way we structure our practice of both.

As this process happened for me, I began to notice that my first-grade students studied me very carefully. I became aware of how changes in my tone of voice and posture registered ever so minutely on their faces and in their bodies. I specifically recorded many different children furtively watching me as I sat in the audience at sharing time. I knew, from their observations of me and the ways they adjusted their language and behavior, that they were drawing conclusions about teaching and learning, about adult behavior, about empathy and respect, about leadership. I became much more self-conscious, newly cognizant of their careful regard, and I know that I had not felt this before as a teacher. My awareness of the children I taught had changed from one of me watching them to one of carefully regarding each other. I think that their careful regard had always been there but that I was simply less cognizant of the intensity of their watching because I had never kept track of the silent but serious ways in which they marked my language and my behavior.

Mami (pronounced *Mommy*), a frail and petite Japanese girl, was placed in my first- and second-grade classroom one September after I had begun to be more acutely aware of the children's role as students of teacher behavior. Clearly, she had been brought to this country and registered for school without *her* consent. Each day her father would bring her to class and attempt to hand her over to me. Mami, pale and sodden with tears, would cling desperately to him like a tiny spider, her thin hands white to the bone with the struggle of holding on. He was mortified at his daughter's refusal to embrace her new school like the other children he saw in the classroom.

At first I tried coaxing, pointing out to Mami, as she clung to him, the other children who had settled happily into our early morning routines. That was without result, and for the first few days of school her father gave up and took her back home. Then we reached a point of no return: Mami had to go to school. The morning routine began again, and each day for two weeks we would repeat it. Her father would attempt to leave, I would coax, and Mami would cling more tightly to her father's neck, sobbing uncontrollably. Then, after he and I communicated haltingly about what to do, he would inevitably begin to pry off those clawlike hands and transfer them to me, at which point Mami would begin to wail loudly and terrifyingly, as if she were about to be sacrificed to some unseen god of American schools. Children would stop work and look up, adults standing in the corridor would peer to see which child was mortally wounded, and her father would beat a hasty retreat as she attempted to run after him and I held her back. Long after he was gone she would scream hysterically, trying to peel those long fingers off my hand and run away; and I, amazed at her strength, would hold on for dear life.

Eventually, exhausted from her struggle, Mami would allow herself to be settled into meeting in the lap of my student teacher, where she would continue to sob quietly and occasionally burst into wails and sobs. This nightmare continued for two weeks. I dreaded it, and it began to wear me down physically and emotionally, as I nursed my wounded ego and a very strained shoulder. Each day, the strain grew greater not only because of the physical battle that this tiny child waged each morning, but also because I knew the other children in the class were studying Mami and me very closely. Although they gave every appearance of being casually engaged in their art journals, working carefully on pictures and designs, there was a distinct attitude of watching and listening. Here were their teacher and a very small child standing off each morning, and intermittently throughout the day, in the most raw terms. It was a very public struggle about deep and private fears and emotions. In effect, Mami was playing out what each of them, at some less spectacular level, must have played out in more introverted ways. Very few children enter first grade without some form of fear and trembling. How I reacted, what I did with and to Mami, and what I said to and about her was being carefully monitored.

This made me wary and extremely deliberate in my responses to her hysteria. I felt as we moved from one day to the next that I had to build a public narrative that spoke about Mami's struggle and my responsibility as her teacher. Each morning at meeting time, a few children would sit near Mami, stroking her arm comfortingly and talking to her in soothing voices. They looked to me for response, as I, also exhausted, carried out the morning routines, and I would carefully thank them for their help. They would question me about why Mami was so sad, and I would turn the question back on them.

Eventually Mami would begin to wail once again, looking frantically at me and the other children as she crawled toward the stairs, and, very deliberately, I would stop what we were doing, and explain that I would have to carry Mami out. My explanations of what I was doing astonished me: They were texts that reflected not the extreme duress I was under and my growing impatience and fatigue, but rather a metacognitive analysis of what my strategy and method for settling Mami would entail. They served to settle everyone down, including myself, and when I would return a few minutes later after locating Mami and my student teacher on the other side of the room with a book, the morning would proceed as if the struggle had never happened.

Once Mami's epic struggle ended, as it finally did, our life in the classroom returned to a normal pace. Mami remained in our midst, silent and delicate, like a glass flower that everyone handled with great care. She gained a reputation for extreme shyness, which the children would relate to newcomers who tried to coax her to speak with them. But no one spoke of her first few weeks in our classroom. They seemed to put that knowledge away somewhere, where silent musings are held.

In October, my field notes recorded Mami's first attempt to share in morning meeting and Andy's exclamation when he saw her get up to sit in the chair. "Oh, you're kidding! Mami's so shy!" Mami sat in the chair, her feet dangling a foot above the ground, and softly read a note that her mother had written in English describing the tiny rock she had found on the playground. The children raised their hands for questions and comments, and Mami, unable to look at any of them, looked pleadingly at me. I whispered to her, asking her if she could say their names, but she was speechless as she sat in the chair wringing those long, translucent hands and fixing me with a desperate stare. Eventually, I called on each child, who would then address a remark to her, which I repeated slowly. She showed no response, her eyes never shifting from mine.

Each week that followed was the same. Mami continued to bring in tiny rocks and crystals, most found around her apartment or on the playground. In early January, she brought in an origami doll she had made, and for the first time she was able to repeat after me the names of the girls who wanted to comment, but she would not say the boys' names. The children, however, had grown quite fond of Mami, treating her as if she were a small doll, showing extreme care to be kind and careful of her feelings.

Small changes in her participation in classroom activities took place. In February she began to participate in movement, which had been a mystery to her. She would stand, fascinated but uninvolved, and watch the boys hurtling through space, watch us all tumbling and rolling, until one Monday when Tom convinced her to play the role of a weight that was supported on the hands of four other children. As she sat peacefully on their hands, she smiled, and the other children almost dropped her when they noticed the smile they had never seen before. The smile grew as March arrived, and we got more used to seeing it when she shared, newly able to call on the boys and the girls without any help from a teacher.

In late May and June, when the weather outside was finally warm, we spent the end of two afternoons a week on the playground, playing what I call gang games: Red Light — Green Light, Capture the Flag, Mother/Father May I?, Hide and Seek, Fifty-two Scatter, and Red Rover. Many of the children I teach have never played these games, and so each year we spend a great deal of time learning the rules and figuring out strategies. Everyone plays, teachers and children alike. This particular class relished the games and would beg to play two or three in an afternoon. Their favorite, though, was Red Rover, a game which seemed to go on endlessly as teams shifted, gaining and losing players. By late June, as school was coming to a close, they would ask only to play Red Rover, and one of their chief delights in this was Mami.

The teams would be assembled, 11 children each in two long lines facing each other. Predictably the game would start with the biggest boys calling over girls who would, in some cases, be unable to break through their line. As the children gained more experience, they realized that a team won the game both by having one of its members break through the other team's chain, thereby capturing and bringing to its side the child of their choice, and by themselves forming a strong enough chain that a member of the opposing team cannot break through, thereby capturing that child and retaining him or her as a team member. In one of our last games, a few unthinking boys decided, quite correctly, that the weakest link in any line would be Mami's little arms, and, when they were called over to try and break through, they would rush at her, breaking through easily, and in some cases sending her reeling backward. I would catch my breath at this, sure she would really break or at least quit the game, and the other children, still watching me carefully as they had all year, would gasp as well, protesting the choice of Mami as a target.

Mami, however, seemed to find the whole thing delightful, albeit painful. She would hold out her arms, checking for scrapes, smiling and laughing all the while. I decided not to intervene in this new strategy, and her team became enraged, holding an emergency strategy conference. The other team stood smirking. They had developed a strategy whereby they broke through Mami's arms, and then selected the largest boy for their captive, leaving Mami as the weak link in the line.

Mami's team, though, rallied around her, placing on either side of her their strongest girl and boy. The exchange occurred again as the aggressive team directed each of their girls to "go for" Mami. But then something strange happened. Mami's link did not break. We were all astonished. Mami's team was jubilant, and the children on either side of her were proclaiming loudly that they had not done it, that Mami was in fact very strong. They rushed over to her showing her how to show off her muscles. She did so, still laughing and smiling. The other team was subdued. They, like I, were not sure what had happened. Was Mami really strong? Or had their player put on the brakes when she was about to crash against Mami's little body? They called a conference.

For their next turn, they called Mami over: "Red Rover, Red Rover, let Mami come over!" Mami had never been called to run over before, since her strength as a link in the line had previously been of no value to the other team. She looked around her, wondering what to do. Her team was miffed, but they explained that she had to run and try to break through the chain of children's arms. Mami took off, running delicately across the field, in a style reminiscent of a butterfly on a summer's day. Of course, she only bumped the line, not really disturbing the children's hands, and the other team, with a great deal of cheering and jumping up and down, triumphantly took her as one of their's.

Mami's former team conferred again. They were sullen and determined. They called her to come over, and she did so with the same poor results, and they were ecstatic to have her back. The other team sent one of their players to break through Mami's arms, sure that the first time had been a fluke. The player failed. A few turns passed. Mami's team seemed to have the advantage, and the game was getting boring.

Then the opposing team called Mami over again, and she ran gently across to their beleaguered line, now shrunk to about six brave children. As usual, she failed, and they greeted her with joy. Mami's team was grim, and they called her over immediately. Before she went, however, the opposing team huddled with her, pointing carefully to where she should run, and giving her quick instructions about how to run. Andy, Tom, and Tony showed her how to get a little speed up. She began to run, a little faster and more directly toward a particular point in the other team's line. As she did so, she threw a smile back at her new team, and they urged her on. Then, another surprise—she broke through. And as she did, a strange look came over everyone's face, Mami included. Thus began a new phase of the game in which Mami could break through any line. Did she really break through, or did the other team let her? I will never know, but we never played Red Rover the same way ever again. It became a game in which Mami was the strategic player, almost like an icon that guaranteed success.

How had her journey as a member of our class, which started so horrifically, ended so well? I believe it began with our early struggle, which the class had watched so carefully, and my very self-conscious attempts to explain what was happening between us and to be explicit about why I handled Mami as I did. I cannot deduce what sense the children made of our early struggle; I can only see that my self-conscious treatment of Mami was reflected in the ways they treated her throughout the year and that that beginning with her became part of how I treated every child. I knew they were always watching and listening, and my status as teacher and adult no longer included arbitrariness or unexplained actions.

The last game of Red Rover provided a stunning example for me of how the children looked at Mami and remembered her tenacity and strength (perhaps recalling how she wore even me down)—and remembered also how they had worked to pull her into our community. The game became a metaphor for Mami's resistance to, and then inclusion into, the life of the school.

In the first pages of this book, I spoke of my wish that all children could learn to "speak in tongues," and I have conceptualized that phrase broadly to include many different kinds of narratives and forms of expression. In the process of learning to speak in tongues, I believe each of us must become acutely conscious of the ways we use language to achieve different goals, some intellectual, some social, some personal. We must be aware that as surely as the language of the classroom is embodied in words, it is more deeply implied by our gestures, looks, and the set of our mouth. Even in a science talk when we are carefully exploring a particular way of talking, how we listen tells stories about what we think. When we begin to see ourselves in this self-conscious way, we use our words and texts, in all their different forms, with clear and careful intentions.

My struggle with Mami taught me that Mami's story — which appears to be a story about community and belonging, much as Jiana and Imani's stories were (see Chapters 2 and 3) — on a deeper level embodies the social principle of language as Bakhtin (1981) characterizes it: "the socially charged life of the word." The knowledge we gain in the classroom has weight because it is knowledge we build within a safe community, where everyone, like Mami, struggles and resists, fails and retreats, but ultimately rejoins the struggle. Together we carefully and self-consciously inspect all the boundaries of classroom life, recognizing that each of us is a link that is inextricably tied to the next.

Contextualizing Language

What we often find as we inspect those boundaries is that our classroom mirrors the world outside. The small dramas that I record each day and the evolution of each child's history within the school provide a snapshot of their place in the world. Thus, as I described in Chapter 3, even in the process of writing them down and recording them, the stories move beyond the domain of teaching or research into the domain of the world, and they carry different kinds of weight. Teaching is not just about the microcosm of the classroom and discrete subjects in the curriculum, although discussions about classrooms often imply that that is the case. Teaching and learning are embedded in the world outside the school, and the children bring different parts of that world with them, as do I. In the classroom, all of our worlds are joined; new discourses are created and different ways of knowing the world are spawned for each of us.

Imani informed Anita and me two weeks before the Christmas holidays in December that she would be moving to another large city on the East Coast. She brought a short note in from her mother requesting that I send Imani's records to her so she could enter a new public school in that city. This was abrupt and devastating news for Imani, as well as for all the teachers and school staff she had so carefully cultivated relationships with over the year that she had been in our school. It was, in the end, a sad event for the whole class because Imani had become our measure of what was the truth in many things we studied. The reader can recall with me Sam's reaction to Imani's revelation about her father in Africa and the children's realization of what a pilgrim was—a revelation that was both joyful and sad in its implications (see Chapter 3). Why did Imani leave? Her mother fell victim to the economic pressure of trying to support three children on a single parent's salary. She could not afford the apartment she lived in, and so had to relocate her children to live with family far away.

As the teacher who had been collecting Imani's stories, I learned from the circumstances of her separation from our classroom new things about how my relationship to the children I teach is always deeply altered through the process of looking imaginally at their texts and the circumstances of their lives. It reminded me of how often teachers have to take the moral outrage, sadness, and fear they feel for their students and transform it into deeper levels of attention to those children's needs. For the children, too, Imani's departure will forever affect their collective history as a class. Just as Jiana (see Chapter 2) continues to influence our stories, moving even into the lives of children she never knew, so Imani has become a specific standard to which we refer in certain circumstances, a standard that has helped us to anchor our learning in the real world. We will remember Imani's stories, her artworks, her dances, and her beautiful songs. Just as Jiana made us multilingual storytellers, so Imani made us bilingual in our own native language. The cadence and rhythm of her speech are buried in each child's memory, and the value we placed on her stories will become part of each child's repertoire as perceivers and tellers of their own stories.

Yet Imani has left a big hole in our lives that goes beyond her physical and emotional absence. Because we knew her stories about her life in Africa and her new life in the United States, we understood the sense she made of the subjects she studied. Her stories, like those of all the children, were public stories, elicited in public conversations throughout the year, and while they served to contextualize the curriculum for Imani and gave it more meaning in her life, those conversations also changed how each child viewed his or her own learning. As Bakhtin (1984) says:

> Life by its very nature is dialogic. To live means to participate in dialogue: to ask questions, to heed, to respond, to agree, and so forth. In this dialogue a person participates wholly . . . with his eyes, lips, hands, soul, spirit, with his whole body and deeds. He invests his entire self in discourse, and this discourse enters in the dialogic fabric of human life, into the world symposium. (1984, p. 293)

All of us participated at some level in portions of those conversations, hearing and responding to Imani's stories and sharing our own. Eventu-

ally, all our stories blend together and the things we study as a community
are understood in a collective way. When the subjects of the curriculum
are contextualized, are grounded in each child's experience both in and
out of school, and when room is made for those narratives to be fully
articulated and shared, the result is a widely applied kind of knowledge
that has deep meaning in the children's lives.

Exploring Multiple Texts

All the children I teach struggle to locate themselves in the subject
matter they study and in the community of the classroom. My role as their
teacher is to help them find the link between inner and outer knowledge,
to place their lives and the vast amounts of information they have stored
about their world in the same domain as the knowledge offered up by
teachers in schools. We do this by nurturing our ability to speak in
tongues, so that the parts of our experience that are unspeakable can find
voice in other forms, so that the "embarrassing footnotes," the deep and
seminal and sometimes painful experiences that inform our private selves,
can move toward the center of our lives as learners. We do this through
the creation of shared texts, through the poems, songs, dances, and drawings that arise out of our expressive action, many of which I have described
in this book and some of which I am sure we have not conceived of; and
we give these texts meanings that reflect the intermingling of our respec-
tive lives. Those kinds of texts are never forgotten.

Time passes, new forms of texts are created, those texts become part
of our communicative repertoire, and the languages of learning expand.
The stories in this book reflect both the joy and the pathos that live below
the surface of our experience in a classroom where children are encouraged
to create their own ongoing narratives and to give their work in the classroom broader contexts and different forms and meanings. Classroom life
is filled with joy and pathos. These dichotomies, though, usually defy
description to anyone who does not teach. The stories here to a great
extent reflect those extremes and describe how, in studying them, teachers
can transform the life of the classroom. This is a hard point to make. How
can descriptions of pain, suffering, and joy change teaching?

Teachers' and children's stories are laden with meaning and value
judgments. They are often emotive and sometimes disturbing, yet they
present truthful renderings of the life of the classroom. Truth, however,
carries with it implications of some kind of absolute knowledge, and, just
as we are at times inclined to question the truth of a child's outlandish or
horrifying story, preferring rather to believe that it is the result of an
active imagination, so we question the "truth" of our own stories as teach-

ers. Truth is something that can be objectively proved or verified, perhaps even replicated in another situation.

If Christopher, a handsome, privileged, blond boy, relates a horrifying story about what happens in his home at night, relates it not just to me but to all his classmates at a class meeting, we reel with the weight of the story. Each of us looks away and hopes the story will end. If the teacher interrupts the child's story, as I have done in the past, and says it is not appropriate for school, or says that perhaps it *seems* that way to the child, then all of us begin to discount the truth in the stories, all of us learns to look the other way when we see or hear something that is unsettling. A value is placed on what kinds of stories are "true" for the classroom, and that value then permeates the kind of conversations, the kind of intensity, the kind of depth that the course of learning will take in any particular classroom.

If I recognize, however, that children's stories are making statements about how they understand their world, that conviction sways the course of my teaching, takes it in new directions and deepens its impact for the children. So, too, as teachers move into positions of personal authority where they believe that the events they witness in their classrooms, *if documented*, provide persuasive records of the kinds of complex and varied work that children can undertake when offered broad expressive opportunities, the tone and intent of conversations about education also change.

I believe that all effective teachers are incipient researchers who use a research perspective in intuitive ways. When these intuitive ways are formally recognized for their importance and for the kind of knowledge they represent, *and then are documented*, they result in the kinds of data I have cited from my classroom throughout the book. The voice of the teacher, when situated in an attitude of wonder and inquiry, when framed with the idea of making sense of the classroom, automatically creates a new culture in the educational community: one in which "not knowing" is equally as valuable as knowing, one in which the questions to be asked are not always clear, a culture where teachers learn to rely on one another for new ways to make sense of the sense children are making.

It is my recognition of and commitment to the importance of stories about learning and teaching that have prompted me to tell them here. Yet children's stories about their world are seen, heard, retold, and mused over on a daily basis *only* by their teachers, and often those stories are continuous, one piggybacking on the next and slowly unfolding as more complete texts over weeks, and even months. If left undocumented and unexplored, they cannot be reclaimed as a way to deepen our understanding of how children construct their intellectual and social histories and to understand how we, as teachers, can teach better.

This book, then, becomes a challenge to teachers to carefully and deliberately gather the children's stories and their own; to offer expansive opportunities for expression of those stories; to follow the tracks the children leave, and to present those landscapes of learning in more public ways. It offers a challenge to the research community to look carefully at the stories teachers uncover and to consider the ways in which teacher knowledge articulates a more complete picture of the teaching and learning process. In this way, when teachers' stories are weighted equally with the body of knowledge coming from the research community, a larger and more powerful picture of how children learn, and the contexts which best foster that learning, can be obtained.

References

Aardema, V. (1975). *Why mosquitoes buzz in people's ears*. New York: Scholastic, Inc.

Ashton-Warner, S. (1963). *Teacher*. New York: Simon & Schuster.

Bakhtin, M. M. (1981). *The dialogic imagination*. Austin: University of Texas Press.

Bakhtin, M. M. (1984). *Problems of Dostoevsky's poetics*. (Caryl Emerson, Ed. & Trans.). Minneapolis: University of Minnesota Press.

Bakhtin, M. M. (1986). *Speech genres and other late essays*. Austin: University of Texas Press.

Barnes, D. (1976). *From communication to curriculum*. New York: Penguin.

Ballenger, C. (1993). *Language and literacy in a Haitian pre-school: A perspective from teacher research*. Unpublished doctoral dissertation, Boston University, Boston, MA.

Bernstein, B. (1972). A critique of the concept of compensatory education. In C. B. Cazden, V. John, & D. Hymes (Eds.), *Functions of Language in the Classroom* (pp. 135–150). New York: Teachers College Press.

Britton, J. (1990). Talking to learn. In D. Barnes, J. Britton, & M. Torbe (Eds.), *Language, the learner and the school* (pp. 89–130). Portsmouth, NH: Heinemann.

Brueggemann, W. (1991). *Interpretation and obedience: From faithful reading to faithful living*. Minneapolis, MN: Fortress.

Bruner, J. (1986). *Actual minds, possible worlds*. Cambridge, MA: Harvard University Press.

Burton, V. (1962). *Life story*. Boston: Houghton Mifflin.

Cazden, C. B. (1988). *Classroom discourse: The language of teaching and learning*. Portsmouth, NH: Heinemann.

Chatwin, B. (1987). *The songlines*. New York: Viking.

Clifford, J. (1986). On ethnographic allegory. In J. Clifford & G. Marcus (Eds.), *Writing culture: The poetics and politics of ethnography* (pp. 98–212). Berkeley: University of California Press.

Cobb, E. (1977). *The ecology of imagination in childhood*. New York: Columbia University Press.

Corbin, H. (1969). *Creative imagination in the sufism of Ibn 'Arabi*. Princeton, NJ: Princeton University Press.

Dillard, A. (1974). *Pilgrim at Tinker Creek*. New York: Harper & Row.

Donaldson, M. (1978). *Children's minds*. New York: Norton.

Fox-Keller, E. (1983). *A feeling for the organism*. New York: Freeman.

Gallas, K. (1982). Sex differences in children's art. (written under name "McNiff, K.") *The Journal of Education, 164* (3), 271–289.

Gardner, H. (1991). *The unschooled mind*. New York: Basic Books.

Gee, J. (1990). *Social linguistics and literacies: Ideology in discourses*. New York: Falmer.

Goethe, J. (1962). *Italian journey*. London: Collins.

Grumet, M. (1988). *Bitter milk*. Amherst: University of Massachusetts Press.

Hillman, J. (1975). *Re-visioning psychology*. New York: Harper Collins.

Hymes, D. & Cazden, C. B. (1980). Narrative thinking and storytelling rights: A folklorist's clue to a critique of education. In D. Hymes (Ed.), *Language in education: ethnolinguistic essays* (pp. 126–138). Washington, DC: Center for Applied Linguistics.

Kipling, R. (1902/1978). *Just so stories*. New York: New American Library.

Leacock, E. (1972). Abstract vs concrete speech. In C. Cazden, V. John & D. Hymes (Eds.), *Functions of language in the classroom*, (pp. 111–132). New York: Teachers College Press.

Lemke, J. L. (1990). *Talking science: Language, learning and values*. New Jersey: Ablex.

Macaulay, D. (1975). *Pyramid*. Boston: Houghton Mifflin.

Merleau-Ponty, M. (1964). *Signs*. (R. C. McCleary, Trans.). Chicago: Northwestern University Press. (Original work published 1947).

Merriman, N. (1989). *Early humans*. New York: Alfred A. Knopf.

Michaels, S. (1990). The dismantling of narrative. In A. McCabe & C. Peterson (Eds.), *Developing narrative structure* (pp. 303–351). Norwood, NJ: Erlbaum.

Michener, J. (1977). Comments on words and exploration. *Social education*, May, p. 377.

Mikkelsen, N. (1990). *Cultural context and the classroom literacy program: The power of children's story making*. Paper presented at the annual meeting of the American Educational Research Association, Boston, April.

Morimoto, J. (1986). *The inch boy*. New York: Viking Penguin.

Morson, G. S., & Emerson C. (1990). *Mikhail Bakhtin: Creation of a prosaics*. Stanford, CA: Stanford University Press.

Paley, V. G. (1990). *The boy who would be a helicopter*. Cambridge, MA: Harvard University Press.

Phillips, A. (1992). *Raising the teacher's voice: The ironic role of silence*. Paper presented at the annual meeting of the American Educational Research Association, San Francisco, April.

Richardson, E. (1964). *In the early world*. New York: Pantheon.

Ricoeur, P. (1984). *Time and narrative*. Chicago: University of Chicago Press.

Rothenberg, A. (1979). *The emerging goddess: The creative process in art, science and other fields*. Chicago: University of Chicago Press.

Wells, G. (1986). *The meaning makers*. Portsmouth, NH: Heinemann.

Index

Aardema, V., 140
Art
  connection between science and, 117–118
  curriculum development in, 119–120
  extending curriculum in, 120–129
  forms of expression in, 111–112
  journals. *See* Art journals
  and role of artist, 115–116
  in science curriculum, 49–50, 130–146
  and thinking, 14
  for transformation and change, 145–146
Artifacts, 5
Art journals, 15
  of "bad boys," 57, 62
  and developmental process, 39–40, 42, 49–50
Ashton-Warner, Sylvia, 7, 37
Authority
  in science talks, 107–110
  of students, 28–31, 48–49, 107–110
  of teacher, 8, 41–44

"Bad boys," 51–70
  case examples, 56–67
  characteristics of, 52–54
  information processing methods of, 52
  language of, 65–66
  and sexual politics of classroom, 51–52, 68–69
  and sharing time, 60–61, 66–67
  and struggle for control, 54–56, 59–60, 65, 68–70

Bakhtin, M. M., xiii–xiv, 5, 33–34, 112, 113, 158, 159
Ballenger, C., 7
Barnes, D., 76, 87, 104, 107, 109
Bernstein, B., 18, 33
Body language, and sharing time, 27, 29
Britton, J., 76, 109
Brookline Teacher Research Seminar, 149–150
Brueggemann, W., xvii
Bruner, J., 2, xiii, xiv, xvii, 76
Burton, Virginia, 107

Cazden, C. B., xiii, 76, 77
Chatwin, B., x, xv
Classrooms. *See also* Community of classroom
  confusion in, 8–9
  as research community, 5–6
Clifford, J., 7, 8
Cobb, Edith, 13, 78
Collaborative approach, in science talks, 76–77, 89, 101–102, 103–107
Community of classroom
  and assimilation of immigrant children, 44–47, 153–158
  developing sense of, 152–158
  and research, 5–6
  in sharing time, 18, 34–35
Compensatory education, 18
  and assimilation of immigrant children, 36–50, 153–158
  and Imani (case example), 37–50
  and Juan (case example), 131–136, 138–140

165